Revision Guide to Year 2 Economics B

Themes 3 and 4 of Edexcel's Economics B

Nancy Wall

Nancy Wall was a teacher for 15 years. Since 1991 she has worked in curriculum development, with a particular interest in teaching strategies and classroom resource development. She is currently reviews editor of 'Teaching Business and Economics', the magazine of the Economics, Business and Enterprise Association. She has long experience of writing and editing resources for students.

© Anforme Ltd 2017
ISBN 978-1-78014-050-6
Images supplied by Shutterstock.com

Anforme Ltd, Stocksfield Hall, Stocksfield, Northumberland NE43 7TN.

Typeset by George Wishart & Associates, Whitley Bay.
Printed by Potts Print (UK) Ltd.

Contents

Using this book

This revision guide covers Themes 3 and 4. Much of the content builds on work done in Themes 1 and 2. Do not rely on this book alone. Every chapter starts with the revision you need to do on aspects of Themes 1 and 2. Build on the work you did earlier. The theme glossaries include only the terminology that is relevant and new for that theme.

Revision guides are good for checking knowledge but do not help much with the important skills of application, analysis and evaluation. So you must practice these skills so you can show a deep understanding of the theory and provide real insights into the way the world actually works. Many questions will require you to draw on detail from a range of topics and themes.

It is quite difficult to do this while you are working on specific topics. But many of the questions you have to answer require a synoptic approach. This means that you must be able to draw on a wide range of theories and examples from across the course, using all the relevant details that relate to the question.

This gets easier towards the end of the course. In this book you will find many cross-references to particular pages where something relevant is to be found. You will also have become familiar with all aspects of the course. So it becomes possible to draw on many different concepts to create a balanced and meaningful answer.

In some places, this revision guide goes a little further than the textbooks, to show the connections between different ideas and current events. Revision guides can refer to ideas from all over the course – because you have at least some understanding of all topics covered. Think about how the many components of the subject fit together.

A word about evaluation. It means *making a judgment about something*. It might entail looking at advantages and disadvantages, or making a choice between alternatives and discussing the underlying reasons for each. Good evaluation requires a balanced conclusion, referring to factors that might contribute to a rational decision. Many of the issues you encounter are controversial, involving conflicting interests and different points of view. Often there is a range of different perspectives on any given issue. Drawing a balanced conclusion requires consideration of different points of view.

If you are comparing two possible policies, you could say:

Policy X would be likely to solve (this problem, whatever it is) but there could be disadvantages such as...

Critics of policy X would prefer policy Y, which would have the advantage of... but might cause complications because...

This is much better than just saying, *there is a trade-off...* Explain everything as thoroughly as you can.

What about Brexit. This creates a great deal of uncertainty for us all. The 2017 exams were written around the beginning of 2016, with the referendum still six months off. However you will still be able to pick up marks wherever recent events are relevant to the question, for example on the effects of exchange rate changes. The 2018 exams may have questions relating to Brexit, requiring analysis that does not figure in this book. So revise the events and opinions that have emerged since the end of 2016.

You are living in interesting times. I hope that your understanding of the subject will carry you through the years of uncertainty that are to come and help you to deal with whatever challenges you face.

Chapter 1
Globalisation

3.1.1 Growing economies

> ### ⚠ WATCH OUT!
>
> Before you start to revise Theme 3, make sure that you have fully understood the content of Section 2.4 in Theme 2, The wider economic environment. This is covered in the Revision Guide to AS and A level Economics B, Themes 1 and 2, pages 84-93. It covers all of the basic aspects of globalisation and trade liberalisation. This book covers all this in more detail but you need to have revised the Year 1 content first. For example, see page 89 on developed, developing and emerging economies.

Extraordinary growth

After World War II, the global economy began to grow.

- In the 1960s, the Asian Tigers took off – South Korea, Taiwan, Hong Kong and Singapore. They began to grow at a rate not previously seen before, anywhere.

- In 1980, the Chinese government decided to engage in international trade in the hope of increasing incomes.

- In 1989, the communist USSR collapsed and the new Russian government increased trade with the rest of the world.

- In the 1990s the Indian government reformed its policies to increase trade.

Rapid economic growth

- By 2000, emerging economies everywhere were industrialising fast. People who had worked in the agricultural sector moved to the cities where jobs were available. In the manufacturing sector, labour productivity was rising fast.

- The BRIC countries, Brazil, China, India and Russia were trading more.

- Even during the financial crisis, the emerging economies mostly continued to grow after a short time. In 2010 both India and China had 10% economic growth. India's growth rate was 8% in 2016. China's slowed to 6.5%.

- Most of this economic growth was associated with rapid increases in the volume of trade. Figure 1 shows how significant trade between China and the UK has become.

Figure 1: UK exports, imports and trade balance with China, 2004 to 2014

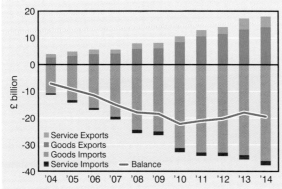

Source: ONS

What happened next?

Slow growth in many developed economies after the financial crisis of 2008-9, especially in the Eurozone, reduced demand for emerging market exports for several years.

● In China, growth was based partly on high levels of investment, some of which was not very profitable. China needed to rebalance its economy and encourage more consumer spending.

● In India, growth now remains high and trade is buoyant.

● In 2014 both oil and commodity prices fell. GDP fell in Russia and in other oil exporting countries, especially in Nigeria and other African countries. Brazil found revenue from its big exports, agricultural and mineral commodity products, declining fast.

● Slow growth in many developed economies after the financial crisis of 2008-9, especially in the Eurozone, reduced demand for imports.

Slower growth

Figure 2: GDP and trade growth 1980-2016 (%)

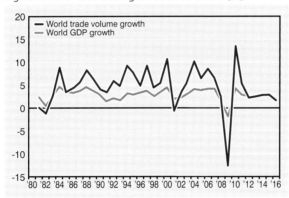

Source: WTO

Watch...
...what happens to oil prices. Observe the effects on exporters and importers of oil.

For most economies, the rapid growth of trade was an important element in GDP growth. But between 2011 and 2016, trade and economic growth rose at a slower and almost identical rate. Figure 2 shows the change.

Uncertain times

Patterns of trade are changing. The reasons might include:

● In some countries, public opinion may shift towards protectionism even though this would reduce real incomes for many wage-earners.

● Brexit may alter trade patterns considerably.

● New technologies (e.g. robots or 3-D printing) may lead to less **offshoring**.

● Ageing populations may need more services and fewer manufactures.

● Political changes and wars may disrupt some trade.

> **Offshoring** means moving part or all of the production process abroad. It could mean setting up a subsidiary company abroad or paying local contractors to manufacture the product or component.

Implications of economic growth for individuals and firms

Economic growth implies dynamism in both labour and product markets.

Market dynamism

● Individuals will have widening ranges of job opportunities and if they are mobile, will be able to increase their incomes.

● The demand for people with scarce skills will be high. There will be a need for individuals and businesses to enhance their human capital. Training may be available, increasing productivity.

● People may migrate from agricultural areas to cities, or to other countries.

● **Patterns of employment** change as businesses find new markets, or fail to compete in their existing markets (i.e. when there is structural change).

● Economic growth may be associated with better health care, education and welfare systems but only if governments take action to achieve these objectives.

For businesses, the big questions is, **can they stay competitive**? Increased trade and interdependence usually makes markets more competitive, so businesses operating in global markets have to watch out.

Businesses in developed economies may improve competitiveness by **offshoring** production to where labour costs are lower. Businesses that are facing competition from other developed economies may engage in non-price competition.

Price and non-price competition

In emerging economies, offshoring by developed country businesses provides strong demand for manufacturers. A ready supply of cheap labour keeps them competitive. Over time, economic growth leads to rising incomes and higher labour costs. Some businesses will continue to thrive by investing and increasing productivity, and by widening the scope of their product range.

Globalisation does encourage mergers and takeovers. These can create scope for economies of scale and for access to new markets. Businesses that merge and then rationalise will shut down departments that duplicate work and cut costs.

Rationalisation

> **Rationalisation** involves reorganising production to achieve efficiency and use fewer resources to get the same output. Merged companies usually rationalise by creating a single department for each function.

Dynamic businesses can adapt to market change wherever they are. Businesses that lack appropriate expertise may struggle. Mobile individuals with skills and flexible businesses will benefit most from economic growth.

Rising incomes

Global labour market

Many people are effectively working in a global labour market. This favours people with scarce skills but hurts those who have few skills and little bargaining power. Overall, economic growth resulting from globalisation has reduced poverty. An estimated 600 million Chinese people have been lifted out of poverty. Similar pictures appear in other emerging economies. Even the people who do not have good jobs have benefited because of the increased spending power that flows into an economy that is exporting successfully.

Globalisation and growth	Gainers	Losers
Developed economies	Employees working in firms that export successfully. People with scarce skills.	Employees who have few skills working in firms that cannot compete with imports and close down.
Emerging economies	People who move from farm work to manufacturing, especially if they benefit from training.	People without scarce skills who have little bargaining power and poor working conditions.

Real and nominal values

Nominal prices (for goods and services) and nominal values (for property or financial assets) are those that are actually in use at the present time, i.e. current prices. **Real values** are stated in **constant prices**, i.e. removing the effects of inflation.

If we want to know how much GDP has increased, it is no use looking at current values. We have to convert these to real values which tell us exactly how much more spending power we have compared to an earlier year. Similarly if we want to know how much better off we are in terms of our earnings, we need to look at real wages expressed in constant prices, not the nominal wage rate that goes into the bank.

> **Nominal value** means value at current prices.
>
> **Current prices** apply to data given at the price level in the year concerned.
>
> **Real values** measure money values with the effect of inflation removed.
>
> **Constant prices** are the prices that would have been in use if there had been no inflation.

Nominal values

Supposing we want to know how much the real price of butter has risen over the past five years. We might know that a tub of Anchor spreadable butter costs £1.75, and that five years ago it would have cost £1.50. What we really want to know is how much of the change is due to inflation. If we have index numbers for the relevant period we can work this out. The formula is:

$$\frac{\text{Nominal value} \times 100}{\text{Price index}} = \text{real value}$$

Calculating: we can make five years ago the base year. If the price index that measures inflation stands at 110 now,

$$\frac{£1.75 \times 100}{110} = £1.59$$

This tells us that something other than inflation has made the price higher by 9p. Maybe the news that butter is not very bad for us increased demand and enabled Anchor to put the price up. The difference between the real and the nominal value of a tub of Anchor five years on is 16p.

Similarly we can take nominal GDP and find out real GDP using the same formula and data from the price indices that measure inflation.

Index numbers

Take a long hard look at Figure 3. If you looked at this in numbers, the blue and red lines would add up to round about GDP without exports and imports. Exports and imports, the other elements in the circular flow of money, are way above the rest. How can this be?

Using index numbers

Figure 3: EU28, changes in consumption, trade and investment, 2005-15

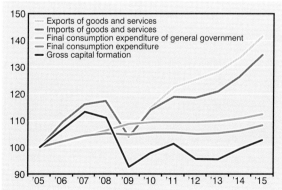

Source: Eurostat

The simple answer is that this is not about numbers or GDP. It is about different rates of growth in different sectors of the EU economy. It tells us about the impact of the 2008-9 financial crisis. It tells us that:

● exports rose faster than imports.

● investment (gross fixed capital) in 2015 was only just above what it was in 2005.

● government spending on consumption (e.g. health, education and general administration) grew faster than total consumption.

● exports rose fast because the weakness of the southern economies in the Eurozone depressed the euro exchange rate, thus making Germany highly competitive and able to increase its export sales fast.

● austerity policies reduced consumption spending below what it would have been in normal circumstances.

Any time we want to make comparisons like this, we need index numbers to highlight the changes.

> ### ⚠ WATCH OUT!
>
> Being able to interpret index numbers is very important. You can compare inflation rates or exports or investment, in different economies. Or you can compare different sectors in one specific economy. These are just examples.

Calculating index numbers can be done like this. The table shows GDP € billions at constant prices.

	2006	2015
EU28	€12,680	€13,500
Germany	€2,516	€2,791

Source: Eurostat

Calculating index numbers

The formula for calculating index numbers is:

$$\text{Index number} = \frac{\text{Current value}}{\text{Base year value}} \times 100$$

Using 2006 as the base year, $(13{,}500 \div 12{,}680) \times 100 = 106.5$

This tells us that the EU28 GDP index was 106.5 in 2015, calculated from the base year, 100 in 2006. In other words, total economic growth in those nine years was 6.5%.

> **Calculate** the 2015 GDP index for Germany. It is quite a lot higher than the index for EU28 GDP. Suggest a possible reason for this.

Figure 4: GDP, 2008 = 100

Companies real GDP growth for 2008

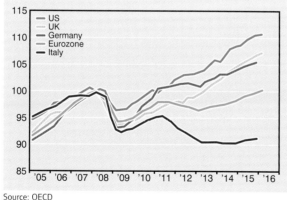

Source: OECD

Figure 4 shows GDP for the US, the UK, Germany, the Eurozone, and Italy.

The base year is 2008 – the year of the financial crisis. It shows very clearly how the different economies fared after that. The outcome is much easier to grasp in index numbers than it would be in raw data.

3.1.2 Trade and growth

● The world changes rapidly. Between 1950 and 2008, world wide, incomes and output grew at an average of 4% per year but trade, exports and imports, grew on average at 6%.

● Much, much more of what we produce and consume is now either exported or imported.

● A significant reason for this is that it has become easier to trade internationally.

Trade liberalisation

In the past, many governments feared that imports might reduce demand for their own domestic products. So they used **tariffs** (import duties) and other trade barriers to make imports dearer and discourage people from buying them. Then governments saw that other countries' trade restrictions were discouraging sales of their own exports. If they all reduced trade barriers together prices would fall, there would be more economic growth and spending power would increase. Free trade opens up new markets.

Trade negotiations between governments reduced trade barriers considerably. This gave businesses everywhere a chance to develop their products for international markets and expand output. This is **trade liberalisation**.

> **Tariffs** are taxes on imported goods. They make the price higher, so that the imports are less competitive. They protect domestic producers.
>
> **Trade liberalisation** means reducing barriers to trade so that economies can move gradually closer to free trade, which means no trade barriers at all.

How trade barriers were reduced

Trade agreements

The past 60 years or so have seen exceptional growth in international trade. Total trade in 2000 was 22-times the level of 1950. Trade agreements that were conducted under the auspices of the WTO reduced many trade barriers.

WTO

The WTO (World Trade Organisation – formed 1995)

- The stated aim of the WTO is to oversee and regulate the international trading environment.
- It has 164 members, accounting for over 97% of world trade. Around 30 others are negotiating membership.
- The main objective is to help trade flow smoothly, promote free trade and encourage economic growth by reducing trade barriers.
- The WTO is a forum for trade negotiations, facilitating trade agreements.
- It also helps developing nations with technical matters and training programmes.
- It provides a dispute resolution mechanism for member countries with trade disagreements.

What it does not do

- It is not a global policeman.
- It cannot 'force' countries to co-operate.

The WTO has its critics

- The WTO has been accused of favouring the richer countries at the expense of the developing ones.
- Some doubt that free trade and liberalisation are the best solutions for developing nations.

Specialisation

Identify products with a competitive advantage → Specialise in this area → Use increased export revenue to buy cheap imports

- It is clear that if all economies specialise in products in which they have a competitive advantage, and export as much as they can, and increase imports from other economies that have a competitive advantage in other products, trade will help to increase total output. When trade is easy, specialisation creates significant benefits.

Trade and growth

- Specialisation leads to enhanced economic growth; GDP and personal incomes increase.
- The link between trade and growth overall is well established. Higher exports increase GDP. (They are an injection into the circular flow of money.)

Examples

India has a competitive advantage in IT services because it has well trained IT specialists who accept relatively modest incomes. So it benefits from exporting these services. The UK has a competitive advantage in the provision of higher education, because of its long traditions and breadth of research experience. It benefits from the large number of foreign students who are, in effect, buying invisible (i.e. service) exports. (Visa restrictions have cut the number of Indian students coming to UK universities from 60,000 to 12,000 per year. Export revenue from this source is falling.)

Specialisation means producing more of the goods and services that have a competitive advantage. The advantage can be enhanced by economies of scale.

Competitive advantage

- Specialisation is linked to the division of labour.
- Individuals specialise and become more competent in their work.
- Fewer employees are needed.
- The availability of finance for investment allows businesses to use the best technologies available.
- The productivity of both capital and labour increases.
- Over time, production costs are reduced and competitive advantages emerge.

Trade liberalisation and economic growth

- Trade liberalisation makes it much easier for businesses everywhere to export. Finding new markets creates opportunities to specialise and to benefit from economies of scale.
- Many businesses (and individuals) benefit if they are adaptable and accustomed to functioning in a dynamic economy, especially if they are able to operate very efficiently.
- When trade is growing, businesses with a competitive advantage can expand quite quickly.
- Some businesses find it difficult to adapt to global demand; they may shrink or be taken over or simply close down.
- These processes are associated with structural change.

Supply chains

Trade liberalisation encourages new and different supply chains to develop. A **supply chain** is a sequence of processes, some of which may be outsourced to other businesses. These businesses, often called B2B (business-to-business) providers, each contribute to the finished product. They are chosen because they are the most efficient suppliers, having a competitive advantage in whatever process they supply. A supply chain in the car industry might look like this:

Designers and researchers → Component manufacturers → Assembly line operations → Distribution network

Nowadays the car manufacturer will probably outsource all or much of the component production, all of the distribution and a whole range of ancillary functions like accountancy, IT, catering, cleaning and so on. Some of this will be offshored. The assembly lines may be offshored, though probably not outsourced, to locations close to the market. (Think of Nissan, Honda and Toyota in the UK.)

Outsourcing

Outsourcing and offshoring have helped to cut costs and given many emerging economies faster economic growth. Each industry has followed its own pattern – Apple offshores all of its assembly processes to Asian countries, contributing to economic growth wherever its markets are, and creating jobs around the assembly plant.

Supply chain management

> **Outsourcing** means buying in goods or services from other businesses, either close at hand or abroad.
>
> **Supply chain management** means organising the sequence of processes that leads to the sale of the final product. The supply chain may have many different suppliers, often located in different countries. Managers must locate the supplier with the greatest competitive advantage so that costs are minimised.

Complex supply chains rely on trade liberalisation to keep trade barriers at low levels.

● They create opportunities for new businesses to grow; by minimising the resource costs of production they open up new markets and spread their expansion across many locations.

● Careful **supply chain management** can make it easier for businesses to adapt flexibly to dynamic markets that keep on changing.

This pattern of global growth is changing. Slower economic growth in China and lower oil prices have already slowed the growth of international trade. Protectionism, Brexit and economic uncertainty may bring more change.

FDI and the link to growth

Growth in incomes and wealth increases spending and investment. As trade barriers are reduced, FDI flows increase as businesses set up factories or other production or distribution facilities abroad.

FDI and growth

● Much FDI flows from one developed country to another but increasingly, FDI is flowing into emerging and developing economies.

● FDI may be associated with the offshoring of production to countries with lower input costs, or with production for foreign markets.

● China invests heavily both within and outside China. It has improved its own infrastructure. It is now financing investment projects all over the world. It is helping to fund Hinkley Point, the nuclear power station that is under construction in Somerset, UK.

● India is now powerful enough to acquire some of the world's leading companies. In the UK, by 2010 the Indian conglomerate Tata had spent $15 billion acquiring Jaguar Land Rover, Corus (the steel company) and Tetley.

● Almost all governments welcome FDI because it provides finance for investment and helps to create jobs.

3.1.3 Trading blocs

Free trade

A **trade bloc** can be a **free trade area**, a loose alliance of countries that want free trade between themselves. Or it can be a more tightly integrated **common market**. A **single market** has harmonised business regulations so that there is a 'level playing field', with all businesses competing on equal terms.

> **Trade blocs** are groups of countries where barriers to trade are reduced or eliminated between the member states.

● The creation and growth of trade blocs has made it much easier to access member countries' markets without hindrance.

● Trade blocs encourage specialisation and open up new markets.

● The best known free trade area is NAFTA (North American Free Trade Area).

● The best known common market is the EU (European Union); it is also a single market.

● ASEAN (the Association of South East Asian Nations) has reduced trade barriers between members and aims to become a free trade area by 2020. It includes Indonesia, Malaysia, the Philippines, Singapore and Thailand. It is working on free trade agreements with other Asian economies.

The single market

Free trade areas are groups of countries that trade completely freely with each other, with no trade barriers, but each member country retains its own independent trade policies in relation to the rest of the world.

Common markets have completely free trade internally and a single unified trade policy covering all member countries' trade with the rest of the world. There is free movement of goods and services.

A **single market** involves free movement of people and capital. Individuals in all member countries can work in any other member country. Businesses based within a common market can invest in any member country. The EU also has harmonised regulations and no border controls between member countries. This could in time make it almost like a single economy.

Trade creation and diversion in the EU

Trade blocs all encourage and increase trade amongst the member states; this is called **trade creation**. After the UK joined the EU, its exports to other member countries increased greatly. Trade blocs also create **trade diversion**. Member countries may trade more with each other and less with the outside world.

Trade creation occurs when there is an increase in the total amount of goods and services traded because of reduced trade restrictions within a trading bloc.

Trade diversion occurs when a trading bloc reduces imports from non-member countries, enabling businesses within member countries to increase sales inside the trading bloc.

Benefits and constraints of trading within a trading bloc e.g. the EU or NAFTA

Benefits	Constraints
● Access to member country markets without trade restrictions means export levels increase.	*For free trade areas:*
	● No protection for domestic industries competing with other bloc members.
● No tariffs on imports from bloc members; lower prices benefit business and consumers.	● Stiffer competition for domestic producers.
● Possibility of economies of scale.	● Reaching agreement with member states is a slow process.
● Spreading of risk.	*For common markets:*
● A trading bloc creates a larger market which attracts foreign direct investment (FDI).	● A common external tariff can increase costs of raw materials or supplies from outside the bloc.
● Greater competition within the trade bloc can increase incentives for firms to strive for efficiency, cutting costs and prices.	● Harmonised regulations may not suit all businesses, especially those without ethical commitments.

Impact on firms of trading blocs

Competing within trade blocs like the EU

● Businesses that can increase exports within a trading bloc will always benefit.

● Businesses that compete with other producers in other member countries will face more competition.

● All businesses will have an incentive to adapt, by upgrading their products, investing, increasing productivity, cutting costs, increasing their competitive advantage and cutting prices.

● In the EU, competition law reduces anti-competitive practices.

● Some businesses may resist regulations that aim to improve working conditions.

Growing interdependence

The growth of trade and FDI has made all economies increasingly reliant on each other. Both businesses and governments are more likely to be affected by adverse events in the economies with which they trade.

Inter-dependence

Figure 2 (page 2) shows the impact of the 2008-9 financial crisis on the global economy, even though the problem began first in the USA and then in some EU economies. For example:

- China's slowing growth rate is affecting demand for exports from both developed and emerging economies.

- Lower commodity prices including oil prices can have a marked effect on the GDP of producer countries, which in many cases already have poverty problems.

- Changes in the macro-economy of one economy can affect its trading partners, e.g. a change in the rate of inflation.

- Brexit may cause disturbances in financial transactions.

Equally, positive trends in some economies can have a marked effect on export trends in other countries.

> **Think!**
> To what extent are the UK and its trading partners interdependent?

3.1.4 Trade policy and trade negotiations

There is a strong connection between trade liberalisation and economic growth. Yet nearly all governments put some measures in place to restrict or prevent trade liberalisation. This process is called **protectionism**; it involves slowing or preventing imports coming into their country. The most common forms of protectionism are tariffs, quotas and regulation. These are collectively known as trade barriers.

Protectionism

> **Protectionism** refers to government policies that protect the domestic economy from imports that compete with domestic industries and reduce employment.
>
> **Trade barriers** include any measure that slows or prevents free trade from taking place, e.g. tariffs, quotas and safety regulations.

Why create barriers to trade?

- To stop cheaper foreign imports from replacing domestic substitutes, leading to business closures and job losses.

- To protect 'infant' industries, small businesses that have started up recently and not yet had a chance to grow. If they are shielded from foreign competition they can grow big enough to reach maturity. This protects jobs and allows new industries to achieve economies of scale. Protecting infant industries may lead to their being able to export in the future, provided they are not protected indefinitely.

Infant industries

- The balance of trade is important. (This is the difference between the amount of imports and amount of exports.) Reducing imports helps to avoid a trade deficit.

- If jobs are lost this is a drain on the economy, there is a loss of tax revenue and an increase in benefits paid. It is also politically damaging.

- Tariffs raise some tax revenue which can help fund public expenditure; this can be particularly useful for emerging economies.

- Often protectionist measures are put into place as a means of retaliation against other countries' protectionist measures.

Tariffs

Tariffs are taxes placed on imported goods; this increases their price to customers.

- The supply curve shifts to the left. (The supply curve rises vertically by the amount of the tariff.)

Tariffs

Figure 5: Tariffs

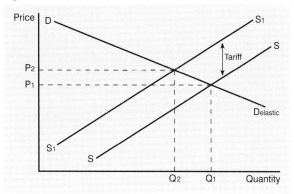

● This causes the price to rise to P2. Quantity bought of the import will fall to Q2. Consumers will do without, or purchase a domestic substitute instead.

● The effectiveness of a tariff depends upon the price elasticity of demand for the import.

● If it is price inelastic the reduction in demand for the import may be limited. This will happen if domestic substitutes are inferior.

Price elasticity of demand

Tariffs are taxes placed on specific imported goods. They are sometimes called import or customs duties.

Quotas are physical limits on the level of specific imports in any one year.

Quotas

A quota sets a maximum quantity of a specific product that can be allowed into the country in one year.

Figure 6: Quotas

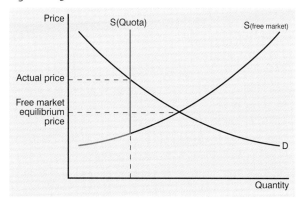

● Quotas make the supply curve vertical at the quota limit. (Supply becomes perfectly inelastic.)

● Reduced supply raises the price and causes quantity demanded to fall.

● The effectiveness of this will depend on the price elasticity of demand for the import.

Other forms of protectionism

● Subsidies can help domestic industries to lower their prices and remain competitive against imports (and be more successful as exports). Governments may think this is too expensive to be of value. In the EU subsidies are strictly limited.

● Keeping the exchange rate low makes imports more expensive (and exports more competitive). China has been accused of keeping its exchange rate too low.

● Imposing regulations such as safety standards can exclude some imports. These are usually used to exclude unsafe products, protecting consumers. Some countries have used them just to avoid stiff competition from particular imports.

Government policies

Costs of protection

● All protectionist measures cause a welfare loss. If consumers have to pay more for the imports they buy, then they have less to spend on other things. This reduces their real income and has a negative effect on other domestic spending.

● Protection reduces competition, which can lead to inefficiency and higher prices being charged for products manufactured domestically.

● It reduces incomes in exporting countries.

● It can provoke retaliation – making it difficult to increase the level of exports.

● Some infant industries are allowed to continue producing rather inefficiently for a long time, charging high prices to domestic consumers.

WTO rules

The disadvantages of protectionism are big enough to make most governments want to liberalise trade. Over the past few decades, trade restrictions have been greatly reduced, and that is one reason why the globalisation process has helped so many countries to grow their economies. Most countries are, or want to be, members of WTO, which means making a commitment to keep most tariffs and other trade restrictions quite low, or eliminating them completely.

> **Trade barriers** help individual industries that cannot compete with imports. But because they cause prices to rise, everyone has to pay more for the imports they need. How much depends on price elasticity of demand.

How protection constrains businesses

On the whole, most businesses favour trade liberalisation policies because protectionism will make it harder for them to tap into new markets. However, a few industries that have faced strong competition from imports have at times put pressure on governments to increase protection.

> **Examples**
> The **steel industry** in the USA regularly tries to persuade the US government to put tariffs and quotas on steel imports. These do not usually last for very long and they usually apply to certain special types of steel.
>
> The **Common Agricultural Policy** of the EU involves a system of tariffs and subsidies that ensures that farm products sell at the same price within the EU, wherever they come from. This protects EU farmers' incomes. It means that everyone in the EU pays more for their food than they would if they were buying it at world prices. (NB the government has said it will retain protection for UK farmers after Brexit.)

Many businesses oppose tariffs

The majority of businesses want to keep trade barriers low. They value the ease with which they can sell within the EU and want to avoid trade wars which might reduce their export sales. Often very specialised businesses need foreign markets in order to reap economies of scale – the home market just isn't big enough to allow this. Exporters of scotch whisky want to sell all over the world – the UK market is not nearly big enough for all of them to survive. They could be greatly damaged by customer countries' tariffs. Most countries have some good domestic substitutes.

> **Show how...**
> ...whisky distillers would be affected by a US tariff on scotch. Use an appropriate diagram and explain the effect on the Scottish economy.

International trade negotiations – the role of the G20

The Group of Twenty was set up in 2008 when the Financial Crisis was gathering pace and threatened to destabilise the entire world economy. It includes heads of government and their central bank governors. The worry was that many countries might introduce trade barriers but in fact all governments tried to avoid this.

● All continents are represented; the biggest developed and emerging economies are involved, together with representatives from groups of smaller countries.

● Initially they met twice yearly, now once yearly.

● Financial and economic stability is a primary concern. When possible the G20 tries to ensure that individual governments' policy decisions are compatible with each other.

● Members discuss policy issues including those relating to the international organisations (IMF, WTO, World Bank).

International institutions

Trade negotiations

Most governments want to reduce trade barriers if trade agreements can be negotiated. The **WTO** facilitates these.

● Over a long period, WTO negotiations greatly reduced trade barriers. In 1994, 123 countries agreed to significant reductions in tariffs and very limited use of quotas in relation to almost all manufactured products.

● Subsequent negotiations on services and agricultural products have been attempted but not succeeded.

● The WTO provides a dispute resolution mechanism that helps trading partners to resolve differences.

IMF

The **IMF** exists to promote monetary and economic stability in the global economy.

● It advises governments on economic policy.

● It provides money for governments that are struggling with trade deficits that threaten to cause very fast falls in their exchange rates.

The **World Bank** helps the poorest countries to develop economically.

● It provides policy advice.

● It offers grants and loans, e.g. for infrastructure development, improving agricultural techniques and health and education facilities.

All of these organisations – as well as the United Nations and its satellite organisations – encourage governments to communicate effectively with one another.

Bilateral trading agreements

Bilateral trade

Bilateral trade involves agreement between just two economies. These have increased in number since 2000. More importantly, regional negotiations have become very significant. These include: the TPP (Trans-Pacific Partnership) and the TTIP, (the Transatlantic Trade and Investment Partnership) which could be important in liberalising trade further. However, there are concerns about dispute resolution mechanisms. President Trump may veto them anyway.

Bilateral agreements make trade regulations very complex because they will not all cover the same issues in the same way. However, only the two governments have to agree, so they can be implemented more quickly than multilateral agreements. They may turn out to be important in the Brexit process.

> **Think!**
> What evidence is there that protectionism is increasing? Give examples and explain their likely impact.

3.1.5 The impact of exchange rate changes

When exchange rates change, there are significant effects on levels of competitiveness, so any change other than small day-to-day fluctuations will affect the pattern of trade.

WATCH OUT!

Make sure you have revised appreciation and depreciation, their impact on people and businesses, and the balance of payments. (See Revision Guide Theme 1, page 12 and Theme 2, pages 92-3.)

After the EU referendum in the UK, the exchange rate fell. Figure 7 overleaf shows how the exchange rate fluctuated between 1990 and 2016.

● Look at Figure 7 and the depreciation that took place at the time of the financial crisis, 2008-9.

● Figure 8 shows what happened in 2016. The high and low bars show the extent of the fluctuations during the month.

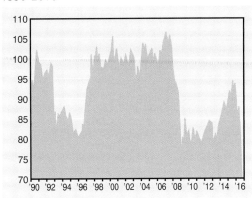

Figure 7: UK effective exchange rate, 1990-2016

Source: Highcharts.com

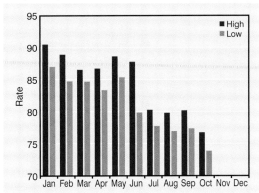

Figure 8: UK effective exchange rate, highs and lows, 2016, 2005 = 100

Source: Bank of England

Fluctuating exchange rates

Think!

How did depreciation affect business? Circumstances in 2008 were quite different from 2016. Explain the differences from the viewpoint of two different businesses.

The current account and the balance of payments

The balance of payments records all transactions between the UK and other countries.

Visible and invisible exports and imports

● The **current account** records all payments for imports and exports, whether visible or invisible (services), plus inflows and outflows of income from investments.

● The capital account and financial account covers all FDI and all financial transactions e.g. when people abroad are buying UK financial products and UK residents are buying financial products from elsewhere.

● Depreciation makes exports more competitive and can lead to a current account surplus when exports are selling well. The reverse happens when there is appreciation.

The **current account of the balance of payments** provides information on trading activities and income from abroad. If export revenues are less than import payments there will be a trade deficit. If we import less than we export there will be a trade surplus.

Economic growth

If the economy is growing, (e.g. when there is a boom developing) there may be increasing demand for imports. Aggregate demand will be strong and exporters may be able to sell most of their output in the home market; they have little incentive to seek out new markets abroad. This may lead to lower exports and a current account deficit.

Depreciation

A current account deficit can be balanced by FDI or financial transactions (the capital account). But if together the outflow exceeds the inflow then the exchange rate will be pushed downwards; there will be depreciation.

● This will make exporting more profitable and provide an incentive to exporters.

● Imports will be dearer and buyers will look for locally produced substitutes which will be cheaper.

Appreciation

If the economy is slowing down or if output is declining, as in recession conditions, the reverse will happen.

Incomes are falling	→	Fewer imports demanded	→	Businesses try to sell more abroad	→	A current account surplus develops	→	The exchange rate appreciates

All these changes will be subject to time lags. The actual changes will depend on the price elasticity of demand for the products involved. Quite often demand for exports will be quite elastic – many substitutes are available. Demand for imports will be inelastic if few substitutes are available in the domestic market.

Businesses that use forward markets to buy the currency they will need in the future at a fixed price will be protected from exchange rate risks until they have used up all the currency bought at previous exchange rates.

Employment and unemployment

● Export growth creates jobs. Import growth reduces demand for domestically produced goods and services and reduces employment opportunities.

● In an open economy that facilitates trade, consumers get many opportunities to buy from producers that have a strong competitive advantage, and therefore lower prices. They then have more money to spend on other things e.g. local eateries and tourist attractions. These will need to employ more people.

● Businesses also have chances to buy inputs from the cheapest sources. This cuts production costs and prices, increases competitiveness and demand for their products, and employment.

● Businesses that cannot compete may make some employees redundant, close down or be taken over. Takeovers lead to rationalisation, which also creates redundancies.

● Competitive businesses recruit more employees while the uncompetitive create redundancies.

● To keep employment opportunities, it is necessary for businesses to strive for efficiency.

Structural change

● This is **structural change** – an important feature of a dynamic and growing economy. It hurts unskilled people who have difficulty finding jobs and also anyone with an obsolete skill. (Welders have been replaced with robots.)

● Changes in exchange rates alter levels of competitiveness and shift patterns of demand, so affecting employment.

> **Structural change** occurs when demand is increasing for some products while falling for others. It can be caused by global business developments that make imports cheaper, and by opportunities for businesses to branch out into new export markets.

The rate of inflation

Inflation refers to rising prices, leading to loss of competitiveness.	If not, the exchange rate will fall.	Depreciation will restore export competitiveness but raise import prices.
Imports look cheaper than rival domestic products.	There will be depreciation as demand for exports falls and demand for the cheaper imports rises.	This may raise the inflation rate, especially if demand for some imports is price inelastic.
Raising interest rates may help to control inflation.		

FDI flows – the short and the long run

● FDI is shown in the capital and financial account of the balance of payments. It creates a demand for the currency of the destination economy. This will push up its exchange rate in the short run.

● If the FDI is being invested in facilities to produce goods for export, in the long run the exchange rate of the host country may rise further when the exports start to flow.

● Appreciation may make many producers less competitive.

● **But...** FDI has potential to increase employment and incomes in the destination economy. This may encourage individuals to spend more on consumer goods, some of which will be imported. Higher imports will tend to push the exchange rate down. This may take time.

Time lags

All exchange rate changes have both short and long term effects. An economy that has lost competitiveness will be helped by depreciation but there will be **time lags**.

● Rising import prices will occur quite quickly – mostly around 4-6 months after a sharp fall in the exchange rate.

● Exports will rise slowly. Most buyers will have already ordered their requirements for at least six months.

● The full benefits of enhanced export competitiveness will take around 18 months or more to emerge.

> **Time lags** are a factor in many economic changes. Businesses plan ahead; they may place orders for their component inputs or products months before they need them. People take time to discover the new opportunities offered by exchange rate changes. (Many government policies take a long time to be implemented and to show their effects.)

The Eurozone

The Eurozone has benefited both businesses and individuals: a single currency does away with the need to make payments in a foreign currency. It reduces the cost of financial transactions between individual countries and saves time and trouble. It makes trade easier within the Eurozone and also for all the economies that trade with the Eurozone.

Competitive-ness

Eurozone members have a fixed exchange rate for all their trade with each other. If any one member country becomes less competitive than the rest (e.g. because of inflation), its export sales will fall. It cannot improve its competitiveness with the rest of the Eurozone by depreciating. Its trade deficit with the rest of the Eurozone will increase over time. The only solutions are:

● Businesses that export cut costs which may mean cutting pay.

● Governments can implement contractionary economic policies e.g. raising either tax rates, interest rates or both.

Both strategies will tend to reduce incomes. Less competitive member countries do not have the flexibility of depreciation to fall back on.

The Eurozone has benefited both businesses and individuals

Chapter 2
Economic factors in business expansion

Terms to revise: product life cycle (Revision Guide Theme 2, pages 63-4), capacity utilisation (RG Theme 2, page 78), economies of scale (RG Theme 2, pages 57-9).

3.2.1 Conditions that prompt trade

There are many reasons why a business might want to start trading internationally. These include both factors that 'push' businesses out of domestic markets and factors that 'pull' them towards international ones. Often it is a combination of both. Most businesses want to expand and increase profitability. Moving into international markets is often the best way to do this.

Push factors

For many businesses the first stimulus to start marketing abroad comes when it becomes steadily more difficult to increase sales in the domestic market. There will be few new customers left to target with their products or services. Sales will come either from existing customers replacing old or worn out products, or by attracting customers away from a rival's product. This situation is called **market saturation**.

Market saturation occurs when it becomes impossible to expand sales further in that particular market. If the product is a durable good, e.g. a washing machine, it may still be possible to sell replacement machines.

Market saturation

Competition

Competition can be fearsome, coming from both domestic suppliers and imports.

● In a saturated market, businesses compete vigorously to increase sales at the expense of rivals. Competition may be based on price or non-price factors.

● Competing businesses will be watching each other all the time, looking for ways to differentiate their products and get a larger market share. Innovative product design, reliability, reputation and clever marketing will be constantly stiffening the competition. Providing value for money will be a key factor.

● This can be an expensive process as it may require constant innovation and/or intensive marketing to increase market share.

Competing on price

● Imported products will often be able to compete on price. Foreign suppliers may have lower labour costs (e.g. in clothing manufacturing). For some products, this will give them a potentially strong competitive advantage.

● International markets can be a welcome addition to the domestic market, as they contain many potential new customers; the scope for expansion and increased profits can be enormous.

Pull factors

Access to new markets in **emerging economies** creates huge potential for increased sales and profits and major growth opportunities for many businesses. The profit motive is often paramount, especially for large businesses, i.e. those public companies that are answerable to a significant body of shareholders. There is a strong attraction to expanding into new markets to satisfy this motive.

Emerging economies are characterised by rapid economic growth. They have seen big increases in manufacturing output and standards of living are rising. Some would still be described as poor countries (e.g. India) but others (e.g. Mexico) are well on the way to becoming developed countries with modern economies. The group includes China as well as many smaller countries like Chile and Thailand.

Economies of scale

- Trading internationally will usually mean that the size of the business will increase.

- This means a greater chance of achieving economies of scale (a reduction in average cost brought about by increasing the scale of production).

- Increasing economies of scale can lead to a competitive advantage: lower costs may make lower prices possible and open up mass markets.

- Sometimes economies of scale are so significant that the most efficient level of output is greater than the level of demand for the product in any but the largest economies.

Risk spreading

Diversifying to avoid risk

- Diversified markets reduce risk: if sales fall in one market, they may still rise or remain stable in another. This is an economy of scale which can be achieved by selling a range of products or a single product in a range of different markets. Trading internationally gives a business greater stability: a problem or downturn in one country can be compensated for by growth in another.

- The wider the risk is spread, the safer the business.

Product life cycle

Push factors

- Saturated domestic market
- Fierce competition in domestic market
- Competition from imports
- The product is in the mature or decline stage of product life cycle

Pull factors

- Potential for increased sales and profits
- Economies of scale
- Risk spreading
- Global sourcing
- Increasing trade liberalisation
- Expanding trade blocs

Possibility of offshoring and outsourcing

- Outsourcing means buying inputs from an independent supplier, rather than producing them in-house. The objective is to exploit possible cost savings. The independent may be more efficient, better able to cut costs.

- Offshoring refers to the process of locating production abroad, usually to benefit from lower wage rates. The purpose of offshoring is usually to cut labour costs but it can also be to produce close to a target market.

Examples

Dyson manufactures in Malaysia. Nike products all come from manufacturers in East Asia. JCB has set up its own factories in India. Peugeot-Citroen, Ford, Volkswagen and Hyundai all manufacture cars in Slovakia, which has a population of 5 million and a tiny market for cars but plenty of cheap skilled labour. If you go to virtualemployee.com you can see how business-to-business (B2B) services might be obtained cheaply.

Think!

In all but one of the above examples, the business is looking for cheaper labour. Which one is different and why?

Extending product life cycles by selling in multiple markets

Extension strategies

The product life cycle helps to explain how businesses might respond to market saturation. An extension strategy is aimed at extending the life of a product either by making small changes in it, finding new uses for it, or finding new markets.

● A saturated market is one that is in the maturity stage of the cycle. Sales eventually reach a plateau and cannot be increased significantly.

● The usual solution for a business in this situation is to develop an extension strategy to prolong the maturity stage by bringing out a new or improved version.

● The next stage is decline, when no matter what the business does, sales and profits begin to fall.

● Moving into new international markets and exporting can be seen as an extension strategy.

● Equally, in a foreign market, the product can be placed earlier in the cycle, perhaps in the introduction or growth stages.

● Market research may be needed to ensure that the product will succeed in the new market.

> **Example**
> This has happened in the cigarette industry. In the UK consumption is in the decline stage; public awareness of the health dangers has led to falling numbers of smokers. Cigarette companies now target consumers in emerging economies where demand is growing. (Note – there are ethical issues here.)

Raising capacity utilisation

● Businesses that have **under-utilised capacity** may make better use of their resources by expanding into new markets.

● Finding new export markets creates more demand for the product.

● Output can expand up to capacity limits without incurring increased capital costs.

● Existing capital production costs (fixed costs) are spread across a larger quantity of output.

● This applies to all businesses with fixed costs – to car factories as much as to small hotels that could interest foreign tourists.

Covering fixed costs

> **Under-utilised capacity** occurs when the business has premises or equipment that could be used to increase output. It also applies where there are enough employees to produce more than they are currently selling.

In competitive markets, some businesses cannot expand sales without cutting prices because of insufficient demand. But if they can find a market overseas, capacity utilisation increases. This helps to reduce average costs, improving competitiveness and profitability.

3.2.2 Assessing the potential of different economies

When a business starts to trade internationally, it will not decide which economy to target at random. Very careful investigation is needed to assess the potential of one location in comparison with other possible alternatives. Much will depend upon the nature of the business and the product or service that it provides.

Broadly speaking there are two main reasons why a company starts to operate in another country.

● To distribute and sell its products or services, perhaps to reduce risks by diversifying into new markets.

The decision is often complex as there will usually be trade-offs between different factors. A country that has an ideal consumer profile may have a high level of bureaucracy, making it hard to set up a new business there.

● To set up production facilities.

Skills

The cheapest labour is not necessarily the best if specific skills are required. Businesses must weigh up all relevant trade-offs before choosing the best location. Some businesses may go for inorganic growth by buying up appropriate businesses abroad.

Organic or inorganic growth

Alternatively a business may set up its own factories or offices or retail outlets, growing organically wherever it feels confident of being able to create a market or cut costs. Or they may arrange a joint venture (see page 30).

Factors influencing expansion into a market

Levels and growth of disposable income

● Economic growth in the economy as a whole suggests that incomes are rising. If demand for the product is income elastic it is reasonable to expect that demand may increase.

● However, it is also important to know which potential customers are likely to have growing incomes. If only the economic elite are enjoying income growth, demand for luxuries may increase but mass produced items may be out of reach for most people.

Market research

● When a business wants to produce close to its market, it needs to become very familiar with that market. Observation of current spending trends and the existing products that are selling well is essential. Extensive market research will be needed unless the launch is designed to start on a small scale, testing the water.

Ease of doing business

The **Ease of Doing Business Index** was created by the World Bank. It looks at a range of factors that make a business easier to start and run, including:

● time, cost and minimum capital required to open a new business.

● dealing with permits and regulations.

Starting up

● ease with which employees may be hired and fired.

● tax payable as a share of gross profit.

● cost and time needed to export and import.

The higher the ranking the easier it is to do business. Regulations are better, simpler and easier to comply with and there is strong protection for business property rights.

Ease of doing business

Easiest to do business in 2016	Least easy to do business in 2016
1 New Zealand	185 Chad
2 Singapore	186 South Sudan
3 Denmark	187 Central African Republic
4 Hong Kong	188 Libya
5 South Korea	189 Eritrea

Source: World Bank

The UK was ranked 7th and the USA 8th. Brazil was ranked 123rd, Russia 40th, India 130th, China 78th and South Africa 74th. Businesses can prosper in emerging economies even when they face problems there, but those countries that have tried to make business conditions easier have seen real benefits and those really near the bottom of the ranking do face serious difficulties.

> **Think!**
> Why might some businesses invest in India in spite of the bureaucracy associated with doing business there? You could take a look at JCB's website and look for content on India.

Infrastructure

> **Infrastructure** includes all transport and communication facilities as well as the basic services such as energy and water supplies. Examples include telephone systems and ports as well as roads, power stations, and drains.

● Economic growth requires infrastructure. Trade requires transport, to bring in inputs and to deliver finished products. It is also needed to bring employees to the workplace.

Transport and communication

● There must be communication lines between buyers and sellers. Basic utilities must be adequate for the proposed developments.

● Businesses that want to develop trading relationships will be less likely to locate where infrastructure is lacking.

● Weak or unreliable infrastructure increases costs of production.

Political stability

Political unrest

Businesses need a stable political situation; civil unrest and wars especially are not conducive to successful enterprise. They may still be prepared to invest but only if the expected returns are very high, compensating for the risks.

● Countries that have a history of political unrest tend not to attract businesses, unless they really do need to be there, e.g. oil companies.

● Corruption can also be a problem and is endemic in many developing countries. For ethically motivated companies this is a problem.

● Both political instability and corruption are hindering the development of certain countries, including some in Africa.

Corruption

Least corrupt countries 2015	Most corrupt countries 2015
1 Denmark	166 South Sudan
2 Finland	167 Sudan
3 Sweden	168 Afghanistan
4 New Zealand	169 North Korea
5 The Netherlands	170 Somalia

Source: Transparency International – the global coalition against corruption

Transparency International ranks the UK 10th and the USA, 16th. Brazil was ranked 76th, Russia 119th, India 76th, China 83rd and South Africa 61st. This shows that economic growth can take place even in corrupt economies. But some businesses will be deterred from locating there.

Exchange rates

Uncertainty

● Exchange rates are flexible and vary over time. This can be a source of great uncertainty.

● Selling exports in a foreign market that has an undervalued exchange rate can be a problem because of the cheaper domestic competition.

● China has often been accused of keeping the value of the Yuan artificially low to boost its exports and to make it harder for foreign imports to penetrate its domestic market. So selling to the Chinese market may entail producing there too.

● Locating production in an economy with a relatively low exchange rate may both cut costs and open up markets.

● However, businesses need to watch inflation rates as well. Wage rates in China have risen and this will affect the competitiveness of goods produced in China.

Factors influencing the location of production sites: costs of production

Businesses seeking low-cost locations are not concerned about whether their products will sell in local markets. They simply want to offshore in order to reduce labour costs.

Low pay or well skilled?

There can be a trade-off between the need for cheap labour and labour with the right technical skills. For routine assembly processes, unskilled labour may be adequate so pay is the key factor. In other cases, businesses look for a location where there are skilled people, willing to work for relatively low pay.

Skills and availability of the labour force

Labour can be a crucial factor in deciding where to produce. Its availability, cost and qualities can all have an influence. The skills and education level of the potential labour force may be important. Experience with new technologies may be needed. India has a reputation for skilled IT workers who also speak English.

● Wage costs can be critical in maintaining competitiveness. China's spectacular growth owes much to its low cost labour force. That may be changing now that some Chinese employees are negotiating higher pay. Some employers may move production to Bangladesh or Vietnam, where wages are lower.

● The workforce may need training; this will add to costs.

● The ease with which labour can be hired and fired is important. If it is easy to make employees redundant, the business will be able to adapt quickly to market change.

● Labour markets tend to be less heavily regulated in developing economies.

> **Example**
> Dyson chose to manufacture in Malaysia because there it could recruit well educated people who were comfortable with new technologies yet still willing to work for less pay than UK employees do.

Infrastructure

● For a business, it is vital to be able to access supplies, distribute goods and services and communicate with stakeholders.

● Weak infrastructure holds up economic development:
   – it slows down the transport system and raises costs.
   – it makes communications more uncertain and difficult.
   – it makes it harder to maintain supply chains and modern production techniques such as JIT.
   – it prevents efficient distribution of goods and services.

B&Q switched its main port and distribution centre from Southampton to Hull to avoid the chronic traffic congestion in the South of England.

● Even in developed economies poor infrastructure can be a real problem for businesses. In the UK, B&Q switched its main port and distribution centre from Southampton to Hull to avoid what is known as 'Southern Discomfort', the chronic traffic congestion in the South of England.

Location in trade bloc

Shifting patterns of trade

Many UK businesses rely on their export markets in the EU. Similarly in North America, NAFTA has created new trade patterns that have cut costs considerably. It is common for businesses to locate production facilities inside the trade bloc where they can access a large market without trade barriers. (Think of the Japanese car manufactures in the UK; they have been promised compensation for losing their EU market as a result of Brexit.)

Government incentives

● Some governments go out of their way to encourage potential sources of FDI.

Business taxes

● They may reduce their business tax rates in the hope that this will attract FDI. This has in the past worked well for Ireland and Luxembourg.

● 'Tax inversion' upsets governments that lose revenue when businesses move their HQs elsewhere.

● When it was first engaging in international trade, China created 'Special Economic Zones' for foreign businesses where they did not have to pay taxes and there were no trade barriers.

Ease of doing business

Businesses that are offshoring production processes to locations with lower labour costs need to consider the ease of doing business just as much as the businesses that are looking to produce and sell in overseas markets. For those businesses that are setting up distribution facilities and sales outlets for their exports, ease of business will be a rather less significant factor because their needs are less complex. See pages 20-21 for detail on ease of doing business.

Political stability

- Ideally, business hopes to locate where the rule of law is reliable. This reduces some business risks.
- If some of the law enforcement agencies are corrupt, the system may fail to protect foreign investors' interests.
- A functioning legal system helps businesses to enforce contracts and payments.
- Some businesses want to locate in places where their intellectual property rights are respected.

That said, many businesses survive in locations where these conditions are not always met. They would still probably be cautious about locations where war and civil unrest are threatening.

Natural resources

- For some businesses, expansion overseas is all about finding new sources of resources that they can exploit.
- Mining and oil companies go to where the resources are and then export them to where there is a demand for them.

- The inexorable rise of China and other emerging economies has increased the demand for raw materials and commodities generally. When their prices rise businesses have a big incentive to seek out new sources.
- China itself has become one of the leading players in commodity markets, seeking out raw material sources everywhere.
- Businesses that need the raw materials for inputs mostly do not need to be near their source because most commodities can be transported quite cheaply. It may be more important to be near to markets for the finished product.

> **Commodities** are raw or semi-manufactured products (intermediate goods) that are traded in bulk and are not recognisably originating from any particular business. Examples include iron ore, cotton, wheat and oil.

Likely return on investment

Ultimately the business must choose the location that will be most profitable in the long run, i.e. the one that gives it the best rate of return on its investment. Forecasting this may be very difficult.

In the early years of China's development process, many businesses located there simply because they thought that there would be profits to be made in the long run. They ignored all the pitfalls entailed in weak infrastructure and political restrictions. Some succeeded in the long run and were glad that they had taken risks early on, e.g. Apple. Others withdrew after years of poor returns.

> **Example**
> In 2013, after 9 years of disappointing results, Tesco abruptly withdrew from the Chinese market. It had created a joint venture with China's biggest retailer, which took over its 131 stores. Tesco kept just 20% of the equity. Most investment analysts approved the move.

While emerging markets are often very promising for investors, there are big potential risks. Bad luck, or insufficient care devoted to planning the enterprise, can lead to substantial losses.

3.3

Chapter 3
Impact of globalisation on global companies

Terms to revise: price and non-price competition (Revision Guide Theme 2, pages 71-4), product differentiation (RG Theme 1, pages 29-30).

3.3.1 Responding to global demand

Globalisation vs glocalisation

Marketing strategies

Some businesses succeed by having a global marketing strategy that applies to all of their operations worldwide. This works well when their markets have similar expectations wherever they are. A global approach to marketing may make good sense. This can be seen as a *'one size fits all'* approach.

A **global marketing strategy** means that the same products and strategy can be used in all markets.

● Producing on a large scale is cheaper, designs can be standardised and there may be economies of scale.

● The product range can be smaller.

● The same marketing campaign can be used everywhere.

● Less time has to be spent on researching individual markets.

● Less time is spent on developing many individual market's products.

> **Example**
> Coca-Cola has a global marketing strategy. Its appeal is such that the company does not want to change its image in any way. So although there are variations in bottle and can size from one country to another, the recipe, the logo, the bottle shape and the approach to promotion is much the same everywhere. Only the language is changed to fit the individual country. This works for Coca-Cola.

But...

● Some sales will be lost if not all segments are catered for.

Negative reactions

● Turnover and profits may not then be maximised

● Marketing tactics and or products may cause negative reactions from some segments of the market.

For most businesses, a global marketing strategy will not be effective. It is likely that some degree of adaptation to local conditions and preferences will be needed. The business will face very different kinds and levels of competition in its various different markets; these will require a differentiated response.

Global localisation

Where markets differ, and they frequently do, businesses need to plan marketing strategies that will fit individual market preferences.

Market segments

● Market segments will often vary in nature, reflecting local cultural norms, fashions and individual tastes. The marketing plan must take account of customers' expectations and aspirations.

● Promotion strategies must fit in with local media availability. Potential customers first have to be identified and then promotion must focus on the media to which those customers have access.

Global localisation means that although the business operates on a global basis, it may adapt or change its products and marketing plans to suit individual countries or market segments. Solutions will vary hugely depending on the product, the market and the preferred strategy.

Adaptation

Global localisation is sometimes referred to as **glocalisation**:

● Sales are likely to increase as each market is specifically targeted. Product features are tailored to customer needs, preferences and incomes. Promotion reflects local media facilities.

● Turnover and profits are maximised.

● Marketing tactics and or products are ideally suited to the local situation.

But...

● The business cannot fully exploit economies of scale.

● Researching each market and adapting or developing products takes time and is costly.

● Wider product ranges and multiple marketing campaigns are harder to manage.

● Average costs are therefore likely to be higher.

> **Glocalisation** combines the words 'globalisation' and 'localisation' to emphasise the idea that a global product or service is more likely to succeed if it is adapted to the specific requirements of local practices and cultural expectations.

There is a trade-off between the very cost effective approach of the global strategy and the painstaking procedures involved in global localisation. Both can work well, in certain circumstances. A global strategy works for Coca-Cola because it is an iconic product, brand recognition is almost universal and the image is crucial to that.

Different approaches to global markets

The Domestic Approach
(Ethnocentric model)

The Mixed Approach
(Geocentric model)

The International Approach
(Polycentric model)

All products and marketing tactics are adapted to suit local preferences and tastes

Some adaptation of products and marketing tactics to suit local preferences and tastes

No adaptation of products and marketing tactics to suit local preferences and tastes: uniform approach world-wide

The geocentric model

> **Ethnocentric Model:** an approach to marketing based on the tendency to look at the world primarily from the perspective of one's own culture. A business believes that what was a success story in the domestic market will also be so in the other countries in which it operates.
>
> **Polycentric Model:** an approach that considers each host country to be unique. Each of its subsidiary businesses develops its own unique business and marketing strategies in order to suit these particular needs.
>
> The **Geocentric Model** sees the world as a potential market with both similarities and differences in domestic and foreign markets. An effort is made to develop integrated world market strategies to gain the best from both of these strands.

Which approach is best?

In reality it is unusual for a business to adopt a purely ethnocentric or polycentric strategy. Most businesses will use elements of both i.e. a geocentric strategy, the mixed approach.

Semi-global marketing

Example

Burberry, with its own iconic product range, did extensive market research in Taiwan. The findings were that Burberry's appeal had two separate elements: one consisted of company history, designs and marketing campaigns while the other drew on Britain's cultural attractiveness. On the face of it, this suggests that Burberry too could succeed with a global strategy, since these facets of the Burberry image could be common to many Asian markets. In fact, Burberry devised a 'semi-global' marketing strategy, because it believed that customers in other countries were interested in Burberry products for other reasons. The strategy was successful, even though Burberry experienced the effects of recession in some markets.

Price and non-price competition in global markets

Adapting marketing strategies for global markets is vitally important to international business success. There are many factors that dictate the actual approach used and these are based around different marketing strategies.

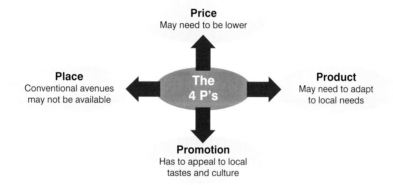

Pricing strategies for different countries

Disposable income

● Price and pricing strategies can be particularly important in emerging markets, where levels of disposable income are lower than in developed markets.

● The level of economic development may not permit standard western pricing tactics.

● McDonalds added lower priced items to their usual products on their Indian menus.

● For some products, such as luxury goods, a premium price is an important signifier of the status of that good and the purchaser as well. This may be referred to as a prestige pricing strategy.

But...

● Consumers are well aware that cheap can also mean poor quality.

Premium pricing

● In such cases prices need to be kept high, otherwise the product will not sell.

● In China, cheaper prices may signify 'fake' rather than the higher priced 'genuine' items.

● A recent survey found that 33% of Chinese consumers thought that expensive meant quality; only 21% of Americans thought this.

Examples

Some consumers use price as a way of judging quality. This happens with both luxury and more basic products. LVMH, the French luxury goods business, sells to people who want status symbols. But it is now changing its strategy for some countries. It found that in Japan, independent importers of their products were charging up to three times as much as LVMH retail outlets charged in France. So they set up their own shops in Japan and decided that prices would be no more than 40% higher than they are in France. LVMH thought they could benefit from the trust that would come from their Japanese customers' knowing that they were not being cheated; the strategy was a success.

Local needs	In India Unilever reversed the traditional pricing strategy of cost plus pricing by looking at what consumers wanted to pay and then setting the price. One of its shampoo products was originally sold for 2 Rupees but they discovered that consumers only wanted to pay 1 Rupee for shampoo. By altering the product they made it cheaper to produce and were able to charge less; sales rapidly increased.

Product

The product itself may need to be adapted to suit local culture and conditions. What sells well in developed economies may not do so well in developing ones.

Standarisation

- Industries with high product development costs and rapidly changing technology need globally standardised products and services; this applies to many electronic products.

- By serving large markets, development costs can be quickly recovered.

- Products such as a Ferrari or an iPad need little adaptation or change for different markets.

- Food and drink products must be adapted for different cultures and tastes. Meat may need to be kosher or halal and beef is no good for Hindus. McDonalds and other fast food chains are very good at adapting to local tastes.

- Technical or safety regulations may be different.

- Products may need to be adapted; in very hot countries car air conditioning must be designed for much hotter conditions.

- Clothing manufacturers need to consider sizing; many Asian consumers are a smaller size than their Western counterparts.

Backward innovation

- Backward innovation – creating cheaper, simpler versions of a product that would be out of reach for people on low incomes – can benefit many people and be very profitable. (Think of mobile phones.)

Promotion

- This has to link in with the potential consumer's culture and background if it is to work.

- Sense of humour can be different as can cultural norms and taboos.

- Promotion strategies have to fit in with local media development and cultural expectations.

- Language has to be accurately translated and images have to be appropriate and not offensive to religious, social and cultural norms.

- The use of celebrities, images and music must also strike a chord with the consumers. Some promotions will cross borders but others have a narrow, local appeal.

- Time and effort are needed to find the most effective promotional messages in a new market. Great care must be taken.

Examples

In many Muslim countries women cannot be shown in advertisements modelling bras. So Playtex used advertisements showing fully clothed women holding bras on hangers.

When Pepsi first started to sell in the Chinese market, they used the slogan that was current at the time, 'Pepsi Brings you Back to Life'. The drink didn't sell well. Translated directly into Chinese, the slogan meant 'Pepsi Brings Your Ancestors Back from the Grave'.

Place

In many emerging economies traditional methods of distribution will not work. Potential consumers may be isolated and distant from shops. Other methods must be found.

Distribution

- In India the Unilever Shakti programme relies on recruiting women to sell their products to friends and families in remote areas.
- At the other end of the scale, in fast-developing places such as India and China, luxury products are sold in opulent and prestigious shopping malls.
- In some countries internet use is much lower and reduces the scope for online retailing.
- Distribution of perishable goods can be a problem in hot countries with poor infrastructure.
- Poor infrastructure can mean supply chains are unreliable.

Example

New markets may have very different methods of distribution. In Mexico, most beer is sold through 'mom and pop' affairs that are little more than private houses with a kiosk on the side or a cubby hole where customers knock for service.

⚠ WATCH OUT!

You can apply the 4Ps to global marketing but you must take into account the variations in incomes, preferences, cultural expectations, product design and local markets.

Branding and differentiation in global markets

Brand recognition

- Brand recognition is key to successful branding. The brand will be particularly successful if the product is obviously superior to others in terms of quality or performance or gives good value for money.
- Ubiquitous brands like McDonalds and Coca-Cola are recognised almost everywhere. Coca-Cola benefits from the fact that it requires little or no local differentiation. McDonalds serves Big Macs everywhere but also serves meals tailored to local traditions – the Geocentric Model.
- Brands add value to the product. In emerging economies, their reliable features provide a quality guarantee; mostly they will not turn out to be faulty as some unknown local brands can be.
- In some cases brands and differentiation provide buyers with visible status symbols.
- In contrast, Unilever creates local brands which advertise the fact that they are meeting local needs.
- In all cases, brands can become very valuable to their parent company.

3.3.2 Demand-side factors in global markets

Cultural and social factors

When a business begins to trade internationally it is crucial that all concerned are aware of any social and cultural differences between themselves and the new country. Being well informed about cultural differences can reduce the risks. Without this awareness costly mistakes can be made through ignorance of customs and expectations. At best, sales will not be maximised.

Values and expectations

> **Social and cultural differences** vary for each individual society. Many groups will have different values and expectations from those of other countries, cultures, religions and political systems.

- In business negotiations
  - It is important to understand the culture of your potential business colleagues.
  - Some cultures believe in directness rather than diplomacy whereas other cultures put diplomacy before directness. (This often happens in Japan.)
  - Some cultures are more emotional whilst others are more reserved.
  - Some are very literal in what they say whilst others are more likely to use coded language.
  - Failure to appreciate such differences can lead to poor relationships when one side gets the wrong impression or feels insulted.

● Different tastes
  – Different societies have different preferences so product designs may need to be adapted to suit the market.
  – Cultural values may need to be respected.

Example
In Asian countries people in business will be expected to spend time building up trust. Respect for seniority is crucial. Holding a business card with both hands when presenting it is a simple way to observe the Asian custom. It is important not to be openly critical of people or situations as losing face is always very problematic for people from the Far East, especially China.

Information and communication factors: language

Avoiding misunder-standing

● Effective and accurate communication is vital to avoid misunderstandings

● Businesses need to recruit bilingual people who can advise them on how to avoid the pitfalls that may be a factor in unfamiliar markets and also to ensure that translations are accurate.

● They will also be needed to ensure that advertising is appropriate to the local culture.

● **Joint ventures** may be created; a foreign business can link up with a local one, so gaining access to experienced people who know the local language and culture. Joint ventures have worked well in some emerging economies. They do not affect the operations of either firm elsewhere.

Joint ventures

> **Joint ventures** involve foreign businesses working together with a local producer. They were made compulsory in China when the development process there was in it infancy. Both businesses benefited from access to specialist expertise.

Example
Tesco has been expanding internationally but has done much better in some countries than in others. It has tried to be sensitive to local expectations by entering into joint ventures with local partners. It teamed up with Samsung in South Korea and did well. In the USA it bought an existing chain, Fresh and Easy, but has not been able to expand nearly as much as it hoped.

Niche and mass markets

● For some markets price will need to be low to attract consumers. Within a mass market, the level of income will be a crucial factor.

● Not all mass markets require adaptation.
  – Mass markets that recognise international brands require the least adaptation (Starbucks, Coca-Cola, VW and so on).
  – There is a mass market in tea; it is often branded but unbranded tea sells well in many emerging markets.

Think!
Would it be worthwhile for Tetley to try selling in India? What would it have to do?

● Some mass markets require considerable adaptation, but are still big enough for mass production to be feasible.

Mass markets

Example
Some years ago, the market for mobile phones in Africa was definitely in the niche category. But then as the masts went up, the market developed because people were buying second hand phones from the developed countries. In time the manufacturers developed new, cheap handsets that could carry a number of accounts – just what African customers needed – and their profits grew fast. A mass market developed.

Niche markets

● **Global niche markets** can grow: the market for luxury goods in emerging economies used to be small, definitely in the niche category. But incomes are growing in many emerging markets so firms that start out with a niche market may expand quite fast.

Examples

There are large groups of very rich consumers in economies such as India, China and Brazil, who value the status that premium priced luxury goods can bring.

Audi has modified the interiors of its sedan cars to suit Chinese tastes. Many business people employ drivers and often share rides with business counterparts, so space and comfort in the back seat is often very important to them. Audi is now the top-selling premium business car in China.

> **Global niche markets** are small, specialised market segments that look for products with very specific features. Producers will usually be too small to benefit from economies of scale so prices will be higher but consumers will be able to get exactly what they want. However they will be able to offer high levels of customer service and will understand the needs of the customer.

● For some businesses there will be no mass market ever, but they can still expand by specialising in unusual products, or supplying business services or seeking out new markets. Adaptation may be necessary to keep the business going.

Example

Red Bee was originally part of the BBC but was bought out and has flourished independently. It made a start in China by landing the job of creating new on-screen identities for Shanghai Media Group, the second biggest broadcaster in China. That went well and so they got to create title sequences and graphics for the 2012 Beijing Olympics broadcasts. They found they had to charge much lower prices and be very cautious about respecting local tastes. But the market for advertising services in China is growing; Red Bee were able to use these successful projects to market themselves to other potential customers.

Niche markets may exist precisely because there are a few buyers who want a very specific product. Then in many cases there will be relatively few suppliers, but they will thrive in a global market so long as the demand is there. These are the niche markets that depend heavily on on-line marketing.

4 P's	Niche market	Mass market
Price	High or premium	Low or competitive
Product	Specialised	Standardised
Promotion	Narrow focus	Broad appeal
Place	Limited outlets	Widely available

Internet sales

Retailing

On-line retailing requires infrastructure – access to the internet and delivery systems. It presents very convenient shopping for both mass and niche markets. Mass markets can develop without these facilities, provided there are shops and market places where people can browse on foot. In emerging markets, many niche products are limited to customers' living locally.

But here's what Goldman Sachs says about China:

Bricks-and-mortar commerce in China is still relatively underdeveloped. And low car ownership limits shoppers' mobility. But with widely available mobile internet, low shipping costs and a flood of cheap unbranded products that could be sold online, conditions are right for e-commerce to take off.

Chapter 4
Impact of globalisation on local and national economies

Terms to revise: multinationals (Revision Guide for Year 1, page 57), lean production (RG pages 79-82), shareholders and stakeholders' conflicts (RG pages 4-6), corporate social responsibility (RG page 6).

3.4.1 The impact of multinational corporations (MNCs)

Growing MNCs

- MNCs are businesses that operate or have assets in more than one country. They are sometimes described as transnational corporations (TNCs) or multinational enterprises (MNEs).

- MNCs have offices or factories in different countries and usually have a centralised head office where they co-ordinate global management – this is where they are based. The other countries where they operate are described as host countries.

- MNCs can be very large organisations with turnover exceeding the GDP of many countries. But not all MNCs are large, powerful corporations; many are small scale by comparison.

- Most of the largest MNCs are American, Japanese or European but countries such as India and China now have large MNCs which are growing rapidly (e.g. the Indian company Tata).

Impact of MNCs on the local economy: employment

MNCs create employment in a number of ways:

- The initial investment for location in a host country creates employment. Buildings and equipment may be needed, creating work for local people.

Job creation

- Once operations commence a workforce will be needed.

- Local businesses may be involved in supplying or servicing the MNC and see an increase in business, taking on more workers.

- All of the local people who have found new employment will spend some of their income with local businesses. This increases local demand and in turn creates more jobs.

- This has a positive local multiplier effect.

However…

- Local businesses may suffer at the hands of the MNCs that reduce their market share.

- They mass-produce standardised products, threatening national product variety.

- They act as agents for cultural imperialism, which replaces and even destroys the native culture with unwanted products and values.

- MNCs cause great damage to the environment by their processes and the transportation of their products. This damage can be short or long term and the resulting situation may be unsustainable.

Wages

> **Take care here!**
> Do not confuse low wages with exploitation of the workers. Wage levels must be considered in comparison with wages elsewhere in the host country.

Pay

- Cheaper labour is often important to MNCs, but many pay higher than the average wage in the host country; there is good evidence that this is worthwhile.

- There are several reasons for this:
  - increased motivation
  - increased productivity
  - lower staff turnover
  - wider choice of workers.

Working conditions

However...

● Wages can be low and working conditions poor. Sweatshops are sometimes found.

● Health and safety conditions are often poor and regulations may be ignored.

● Child labour may be used and exploited.

> **Example**
> in 2010, groups of low-paid employees in southern China began campaigning for higher wages. Some committed suicide, leading to considerable publicity. South Korean, Japanese and Taiwanese MNCs, e.g. Foxconn, realised that the publicity was reaching alarming levels and they would have to raise wages. In some cases, 30% increases were obtained and the Chinese government raised its minimum wage in many areas. The fact remains that world-wide, many MNCs are getting away with paying very little.

Local firms, the local community and the environment

Multiplier effect

New businesses setting up create economic activity all around them. This is what is meant by a multiplier effect. The positive effect on employment (page 32) is just one aspect of it. Other new businesses will develop to offer necessary goods and services.

● Component manufacturers may spring up, offering reliable JIT deliveries.

● New businesses may outsource, using local businesses to provide ancillary services such as canteen management and cleaning.

● Well-organised local government departments may insist on deals that involve the new business in infrastructure development, environmental protection and communal facilities.

● Training may lead to technology transfer. (See page 34.)

But...

● Some local governments, especially in economies that are in the early stages of development, may be quite weak. This may allow powerful MNCs to minimise their contributions to local facilities and to be careless about environmental damage.

● Local businesses may suffer if MNCs reduce their market share. They may even have to close down.

> **Example**
> The highly successful Asian economies that have welcomed MNCs for more than 40 years, such as Taiwan, Singapore, South Korea and Hong Kong, now have the standards of living that we associate with rich developed countries. Innovation and new technologies have taken hold and competition has forced local businesses to become more efficient.

Impact of MNCs on the national economy: economic growth

● The growth of business activity will stimulate the whole economy, provided the MNC recruits local people.

● Increased employment and wages should enlarge the tax base and increase government revenue.

Business culture

● If unemployed people receive benefits, this bill may decrease.

● Increased government expenditure can benefit the wider population and the economy as a whole.

● If the MNC develops a vibrant business culture that includes people recruited locally, the employees it trains may in time move on and help their new employers to become more efficient and successful in business.

FDI and the balance of payments

- Exports may increase, improving the balance of payments.

- As the economy develops more export opportunities may be created, e.g. tourism.

- When one MNC brings foreign direct investment (FDI) into the economy, and succeeds, other MNCs will be less afraid of the risks involved and keener to locate there. Flows of FDI increase further and other new technologies are introduced into the economy.

- With increased growth and increasing wealth comes the ability to spend and invest. Governments can invest in infrastructure, which will in turn generate more MNC interest.

- In time, emerging country governments and business may themselves generate FDI in other economies. India and China are increasing the amount of FDI outflows. China in particular wants to secure future supplies of essential raw materials and is using FDI to do this, in Africa particularly.

Appreciation

- Flows of FDI into the economy, if large, will tend to push the exchange rate up (appreciation). This will make imports cheaper and help to raise standards of living.

Technology and skills transfer

- MNCs may require skilled workers and train up the local workforce.

Increased competitive-ness

- They may acquire useful skills that will benefit them if they move on.

- Locals trained as managers may learn new business techniques.

- MNCs often bring new technologies, techniques and methods which can be learnt and adopted in the host country.

- New work practices and technology help the host country to become more competitive and grow – this is called **technology transfer**.

> **Technology transfer** occurs when foreign businesses locate in emerging economies, bringing with them new skills and techniques that were not previously accessible. Trained employees may go on to work in local businesses where they can pass their technological knowledge to their new colleagues.

However...

- MNCs may not train local workers to a high level.

- Skills may be brought in by hiring expat workers; locals may only get the unskilled jobs.

Potential issues

- Managers are often not recruited locally.

- R&D facilities may be kept in the home country, reducing opportunities for local people to develop skills or technology transfer.

- Many MNCs enter another country simply to access a new market, so only sales and marketing facilities are established.

Consumers

To the extent that incomes rise, consumers will spend more and create demand in the economy. Many people have been lifted out of poverty as they moved from agricultural areas to the cities and their productivity rose. Famines are rare, where once they occurred regularly. However:

Incomes and inequality

- Many people in emerging economies need to pay for education, health care and pensions. They may save rather than spend. Many emerging economies have limited welfare policies.

- Income may not be evenly distributed across the population. Urban Chinese are much better off than rural.

R&D

Business culture

Technology and skills transfer has transformed many emerging economies. China now has many researchers and they are giving the economy an additional competitive edge. Specialisation is working well for China; For example, it has pioneered the development of cheap solar panels. In developed economies, during the 1980s and 1990s, many struggling businesses observed the success of lean production, developed in Japan. This approach will become increasingly relevant in emerging economies, leading to changes in management strategies.

Tax revenues and transfer pricing

● Increased employment and wages should enlarge the tax base and increase government revenue.

● If benefits are paid to the unemployed, this bill may decrease.

● Profits of the MNC can be taxed.

● Increased government expenditure can benefit the wider population and the economy in general.

However...

Where do profits go?

● Profits can be repatriated to the home country.

● Taxation can be reduced or avoided by **transfer pricing**.

● MNCs are likely to take whatever incentives are on offer, stay for a while and then move to the newest low cost location in another country, leaving behind unemployed workers and a weakened economy.

> **Transfer pricing** occurs when one part of an MNC in one country transfers (sells) goods or services to another part in another country. The price charged is the 'transfer price'. This may be unrelated to costs incurred and can be set at a level which reduces or cancels out profit and hence the total tax paid by the MNC. It can move profits to the location with the lowest tax rates.

> **Think!**
> How do governments view the practice of transfer pricing?

3.4.2 Ethical issues

 WATCH OUT!

> Before starting work on this section, make sure you understand the Shareholder Model and the Stakeholder Model. (See revision reminder at the start of this chapter.)

> **Stakeholders** are all those people who have an interest or 'stake' in a particular business. Stakeholder groups include customers, employees, suppliers, shareholders, government, pressure groups and local communities. Sometimes the environment is referred to as a stakeholder as well.

Stakeholder conflicts

Business decisions are based on profit maximisation.

Shareholder pressure

● One way to do this is to concentrate on keeping all costs to the absolute minimum (the Shareholder Model). This keeps shareholders happy but has certain drawbacks.

● Shareholder pressure to maximise profits can push MNCs into cutting costs in ways that are very detrimental to other stakeholders' interests.

● Outside their home country, MNCs may hope to get away with doing things that would not be acceptable within the legal system of the home country.

● In the home country, stakeholders are often protected by Corporate Social Responsibility (CSR) standards. But in many emerging economies regulatory standards are much lower than they are in the developed world.

Low pay

● Many contract suppliers are pressed by MNCs to accept low prices. They make this possible by offering employees very low pay. Some get away with this approach.

● When these things happen the businesses concerned may face reputation issues.

Example

When BP leased the Deepwater Horizon drilling rig to extract oil from beneath the Gulf of Mexico, it had the best intentions. Theirs was the deepest oil well in history, over 1000m under the sea and 10,685m beneath the seabed. It blew up in 2009, killing 11 people and creating a massive oil slick. BP had hired many sub-contractors to help with the work but ultimately, BP was responsible for the safe running of the project. Many people came forward to say that basic safety procedures had at times been neglected. The causes of the accident were found to lie in a whole series of relatively small errors that had occurred because efforts were being made to cut costs and maximise profit.

The stakeholders

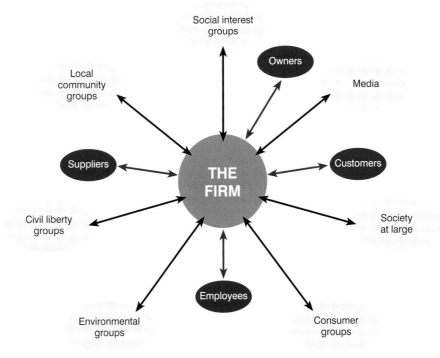

There is an alternative approach – to treat employees as assets and customers' welfare as paramount (the Stakeholder Model). This involves **ethical decision making**.

> **Ethical decision making** means following codes of practice that embody moral values. The objective is to do the right thing, acting with honesty and integrity and taking into consideration the interests of everyone affected by the decision.

● The stakeholder approach involves considering the interests of stakeholders, but ethical business goes further in using clearly defined moral values as a basis for a consistent approach, based on what is right.

Ethical business

● Ethical business involves basing decisions on a set of clearly defined moral principles, and striving to do the right thing regardless of purely commercial considerations.

● This does include many elements of CSR but it goes beyond that in a deliberate attempt to operate on the basis of declared moral values.

● CSR may go no further than scrupulously observing the law in the country of operation. Ethical decision-making recognises that the law may not necessarily protect the interests of all stakeholders and therefore the business must set its own standards.

● Businesses that follow this approach will be rigorous and consistent in their decision-making.

Pay and working conditions

MNC pay

Pay and working conditions	● Should businesses improve pay and conditions? ● There is a trade-off between standards of pay and conditions and employee morale and productivity. This has to be weighed against increased costs.

Inevitably, pay and working conditions are usually better in developed economies. In many emerging economies, large numbers of jobs are created but some involve working very long hours for low pay. Some also involve working in hazardous conditions. Working for MNCs directly will usually mean that pay and working conditions will be better than in local businesses but not as good as in the developed economies.

Environmental considerations

The environment	● Should businesses protect the environment? ● All businesses affect the environment in some way by their activities. There may be a trade-off between controlling such problems as emissions and pollution and keeping costs down.

Sustainability vs. costs

Local regulations on greenhouse gas emissions are often much weaker than they are in the developed world. Facilities for safe waste disposal may be very poorly organised. Most countries could improve upon their existing arrangements. Mining activities are particularly damaging; they may involve displacing people who depend on income from farming and ruin the area by dumping toxic waste. Some activities are unsustainable – e.g. forest clearance for palm oil production. This could be solved if all MNCs required oil palms to be cultivated sustainably.

Local regulations on greenhouse gas emissions are often much weaker than they are in the developed world.

Think!

1. Explain why it is difficult to reduce carbon emissions quickly.

2. Some of the energy used to manufacture Apple products in China will come from coal fired power stations. If China decided to ban the use of coal, how would Apple react and how would customers be affected?

3. How might governments adopt a fair way to address the problem?

Supply chain considerations

- In the globalised economy many businesses offshore parts of their production process. If they do this by contracting with local suppliers to manufacture the products that they will sell, they may have very little control over working conditions. The contractors may be paid very little for their output and this will make it hard for them to pay a reasonable wage or to improve working conditions. This will lead to **exploitation of labour**.

Child labour

- Child labour is still to be found in many very poor countries. It is not ethical for MNCs to allow this. All will say that they stipulate no use of child labour in their contracts. But then they have to enforce it, which is not easy. Some will turn a blind eye and hope that they are not found out. These issues are commonly found in garment manufacturing.

> **Exploitation of labour** means paying employees less than the value of what they produce. Employers who pay less than the amount of revenue generated by the employee are abusing the power that they have in labour markets where there are more people looking for work than jobs available.

Marketing considerations

- Product labelling and promotion generally should not mislead consumers or offend cultural communities.

- It should be meaningful and appropriate for the culture prevailing in the relevant market.

Advertising standards

- Promotion may suggest consumer benefits that are not actually likely to materialise.

- In developed economies advertising standards including product labelling are regulated but this may not happen in emerging economies.

- MNCs should take great care to understand their target markets and act on their findings.

Ethical behaviour and profitability

There may appear to be a trade-off between ethical behaviour and profitability but the reality is more complex.

- Behaving ethically is likely to increase costs and reduce profitability in the short run.

- Some of the most profitable companies are way down ethical rankings.

- Yet many high ranked ethical companies make good profits.

Reputation

- Ethical behaviour can enhance company reputations and increase profitability, creating a competitive advantage.

- Cutting costs can benefit shareholders; it may also allow price cuts, so raising real incomes.

It is becoming very difficult to identify big businesses that can reasonably claim to prioritise ethical behaviour. Many have introduced certain ethical practices but have later been found to be decidedly unethical in some other context. A number of ethical rankings have been produced, often containing companies that appear to have been ethically wanting in certain respects. Those identified as ethical include Unilever, Proctor and Gamble, Kraft Foods, Hewlett Packard, Marks and Spencer, Aldi and Dell, among many others. None of these is amongst the world's 10 most profitable companies.

> ⚠ If you are asked about ethical issues in the exam, it is important to include both sides of the argument and present a balanced answer with examples.

Are MNCs a force for good?

MNC impact

Good	Bad
• Creates FDI	• Illegal and unethical behaviour
• Brings jobs	• Exploitation of labour – low wages, poor working conditions, lack of health and safety, child labour
• Regional multiplier effect	
• Skills and technology transfer	
• Increased demand for local businesses/suppliers	• Environmental degradation/pollution
	• Unsustainable practices
• Increased tax revenues – Government has more revenue to spend	• Tax avoidance
	• 'Race to the bottom'
• Export earnings	• Cultural imperialism
• Other MNCs may follow	• Local businesses pushed out
• CSR policies bring benefits	• Profits repatriated and not put back into local economy

3.4.3 Controlling MNCs

● By their very nature MNCs are hard to control because they transcend national boundaries.

● There is no such thing as a 'world government' or 'world court' that can prevent MNCs from doing what they want or force them to modify their behaviour.

● Many emerging economies lack the strong legal institutions and regulations that are needed to protect both consumers and employees.

Pressure groups

In practice, keeping MNCs under control often requires a *combination* of factors. Public opinion can lead to the creation of **pressure groups** that may mount media campaigns to persuade an MNC to modify its actions. Governments can be persuaded to intervene, or start legal proceedings. However, the effectiveness of these factors in controlling MNCs varies according to circumstances.

Political influence and legal control

● Politicians are usually aware of the damage that MNCs can do. Where the **legal system** is strong and **labour law** is enforced, action can be taken.

Legal controls

● There are international organisations such as the UN International Labour Organisation (ILO) that sets global standards for **working conditions**. The OECD's Guidelines on Multinational Enterprises provides advice for developed country governments.

● **Trade unions** vary in their strength when confronting MNCs but they exist to protect their members and they can hold MNCs to account if they do not comply with established regulations.

But...

● The **size and the power of the host government** matters. China is likely to be much more effective in controlling MNC behaviour than say, Zambia or Madagascar. Some governments are desperate for FDI and overlook low pay and poor working conditions. Governments that face very weak opposition may choose to ignore harsh treatment of employees and environmental damage.

● **Size of the MNC:** larger companies can be less susceptible to outside pressure. They can afford better publicists, PR agents and legal teams.

● **Importance of the MNC to the host country:** smaller or emerging economies may be reluctant to confront a company that may be important to it both economically and in terms of employment. National objectives may override concern for local communities. These economies may anyway have very light regulatory systems. Trade unions may be weak.

Pressure groups and social media

> **Pressure groups** are organisations that attempt to influence public policy and especially government legislation, regarding their particular concerns and priorities.

Pressure groups have existed for many years. Oxfam was set up in 1942 with the name, Oxford Committee for Famine Relief. Nowadays it still tackles natural disasters and operates in war zones but it also seeks to work with MNCs. The objective is to improve MNCs' working conditions, which can of course help the business to become more ethical and improve its image and reputation.

Social media has given pressure groups opportunities to reach out into wider communities. It helps pressure groups to stay in close touch with their supporters. Social media also mobilises public opinion and focuses attention on specific situations.

The impact of pressure groups and social media varies:

● **The strength of public opinion** and the level of public awareness, the number of people who are concerned and the depth of their feelings all affect the degree of influence that public opinion can have.

Public opinion

● **The degree to which public opinion matters to the MNC** will be important. A company that relies on consumers for its sales is more likely to be influenced by tactics such as protests and boycotts than one that supplies other businesses.

● **Social media and the internet** can work both ways! Businesses use it to promote their products and to boost their own image.

● **Some pressure groups have more strength and vigour** than others; their campaigns may be more effective. Greenpeace is renowned for its direct actions and headline grabbing stunts.

> **Example**
> Shell has been widely criticised for the way it has treated local communities in Nigeria. It has tried to improve matters and may have dealt with the worst problems. But people living near the oil wells still have to contend with widespread environmental degradation and the criticism continues. Shell may be losing sales revenue because some potential customers will not buy their petrol if they can avoid it.

The table on page 41 summarises the range of factors that may exert an influence on MNCs.

Self-regulation

Attempts to control MNCs have had some success. They have made it imperative for many MNCs to think about the impact of their operations. Many are making some attempt to limit the negative impact they have on people who have little power to protect themselves. However, some MNCs simply make a show of concern and set up programmes that have a very small impact on the people affected. Constant vigilance is required to expose the facts and counter exaggerated claims, on both sides.

CSR

The idea of corporate social responsibility has made MNCs concerned for their image and reputations. MNCs tend to fall into three groups

● Those that really care about their employees and make sure that pay and conditions are good.

● Those that value their image and reputation and make some genuine effort to show that they want to avoid scandals associated with very low pay and bad working conditions.

● Those that make minimal practical effort to safeguard their workers in any way.

Almost all MNCs say that they comply with the local law wherever they are located. Those that work with their own employees will usually make some effort to protect them. A problem arises when MNCs are sub-contracting production to local suppliers. This is often cheaper than setting up their own production facilities. It cuts costs but this can mean that the suppliers' employees get very low pay. Many MNCs instruct their suppliers not to use child labour, but some then turn a blind eye.

Factors that can control the behaviour of MNCs

Agent	Description	Example
Public Opinion	The way people feel about a company can influence its actions. If the public decide not to buy a certain product or brand because they disapprove of the company's actions it can persuade them to change policies.	The boycott of Nestlé is the world's longest running. It began in 1977 in response to aggressive marketing of Nestlé baby milk formula in poorer countries. Public concern over phone hacking by the media led to the closure of the News of the World.
Pressure Groups	An organised group that seeks to influence either the political and legal process or whole industries or individual companies. **Pressure groups** can organise campaigns, protests or even direct action.	Greenpeace campaigns for environmental causes. *Action on Smoking and Health* (ASH) is a campaigning public health charity that works to eliminate the harm caused by tobacco. Tescopoly is concerned with the negative impact of supermarkets' power and Tesco in particular.
Social Media and the Internet	More and more campaigns aimed at affecting the behaviour of MNCs make use of the internet and sites such as Facebook and Twitter. These speed up the flow of information and can make the actions of groups and individuals much more effective.	SOMO is an organisation which investigates multinational corporations and the consequences of their activities for people and the environment around the world. It uses Twitter, Facebook and YouTube to spread its information and campaigns.
The Media	Newspapers and TV programmes can mount campaigns to mobilise public opinion and affect MNCs' behaviour.	The BBC Panorama programme investigated working conditions in Primark's supply chain.
Self-regulation	Many MNCs follow a code of conduct which sets their own standards of behaviour. This may be because of altruism or to prevent adverse criticism.	Multinational seed companies, Emergent Genetics and Proagro, have launched a scheme of incentives and disincentives to persuade their suppliers to discontinue the use of child labour on their farms.
Government Control & Regulation	Governments can set up regulatory bodies to monitor the behaviour of businesses or industries. They can have advisory or legally enforceable powers. Governments can insist that MNCs form joint ventures.	In the UK the Competition and Markets Authority (CMA) has far reaching powers to investigate a business or industry. For a time, China insisted on joint ventures for FDI projects.
Legal enforcement	All countries have legal codes, i.e. laws, and MNCs that break them are subject to prosecution.	National Minimum Wage Act, Health and Safety at Work Act and similar laws in other countries.
Shareholder Groups	Shareholders who are the owners of a business can try to affect an MNC's behaviour by protest or votes at the AGM.	BP shareholders mounted a rebellion and protest at BP's AGM over its plans for Canada's oil sands.

Boycotts

Environmental issues

Regulation

Laws

3.5

Chapter 5
Global labour markets

Terms to revise: structural change (Revision Guide Theme 2, page 103), interdependence (pages 9-10 in this book), recession (RG Theme 2, pages 94-6), capital intensive production (RG Theme 2, page 77).

3.5.1 Employment patterns

The global labour market refers to everyone who is seeking work the world over. As with the domestic labour market, it is made up of all those who supply labour and all those who demand it.

Growth of the global labour force

Rural to urban

- There has been a mass movement from the rural areas to the cities, with more than one billion people entering the global labour force. This has been the basis of the rise of the Chinese economy, lifting hundreds of millions of people out of poverty.

- Others have been moving into the service sector, meeting all kinds of demand, e.g. for health and social care, cooked food and recreational activities.

- People seeking work may compete with labour in other countries through trade and through migration.

For example:

- Garment makers in Europe will compete with garment makers elsewhere who are exporting.

- Businesses that cannot recruit in their domestic market because of skill shortages will recruit overseas.

The global supply of labour almost doubled in absolute numbers between the 1980s and early 2000s, with half of that growth coming from Asia. It was estimated to be 1.7 billion in 1980, 2.9 billion in 2010.

- At the same time, the rate at which new workers entered the workforce in the developed economies began to decline due to lower birth rates.

- It is difficult to gain accurate figures but the global labour force in 2015 was around 3 billion, with unemployment of about 208 million.

Competition

- It is estimated that the global labour force will have increased to 3.5 billion by 2030. An increase in the supply of labour makes the labour market more competitive and for some, reduces incomes.

Structural change

> **Structural change** occurs when resources are being reallocated. Where demand for a specific product is falling, the demand for labour will diminish. Where new products are coming onto the market and selling well, employers will demand more labour. Changes in consumer preferences and new technologies will change employment patterns too.

- The structure of the global labour force is constantly changing.

Low skill means low pay

- In the more developed and richer countries competition from the millions of new low skilled workers abroad has depressed wages for the domestic low skilled workers.

- Wherever possible, people will move from areas where pay is low to places where wages are higher, trying to improve their standard of living.

- As technology has improved in more advanced economies, the demand for skilled workers has increased faster than the ability of the education and training system to supply them and this has pushed up pay for those with scarce skills.

- In India and China, 70% and 35% respectively have no more than primary education. But still there are large numbers of skilled people there who are available for work

● A report by the McKinsey Global Institute predicts that this will change dramatically over the next two decades and that these two countries will add 184m graduates to the global labour market. Even so, China will still need 40 million more graduates than it can produce at present.

Skill shortages

● In developed economies the big change is the rapidly ageing and shrinking workforce. This will need to be compensated by improvements in productivity.

● Low skilled labour cannot replace all these people and McKinsey (the consultancy) predicts that there will be a global surplus of 90 million such workers.

Interdependence of labour markets

● Individual labour markets are becoming more and more interconnected and as a result, interdependent. As globalisation spreads and economies become more integrated so too do labour markets.

● Trade liberalisation and the creation of trade blocs also make it easier for workers to move between labour markets.

Labour mobility

● A shortage of labour in the NHS in 2014 led to managers recruiting 6,000 nurses from overseas. This has implications for the labour markets from which they came: there may be skill shortages there.

● Changes in one economy will lead to changes elsewhere. The availability of cheap and sometimes skilled labour in emerging economies will affect the supply of labour in the developed economies.

● What happens in one part of the global labour market has an impact on other areas. Workers willing to accept lower wage rates abroad have a dampening impact on wage rates in the domestic economy.

● Political changes may reverse some of these trends in the next 10 years, though probably not in ways that will make people better off.

In your own words...
Explain the benefits of global structural change and the disadvantages. Compare your analysis with someone else's and consider the implications of any differences.

3.5.2 Wage rates

Factors that influence the supply of and demand for labour

Supply of labour	Birth and mortality rates – low in developed economies and parts of Asia. – falling but still high in Africa, India and others. Education and skills training – human capital. Women's rate of participation in the labour market. Ease of migration.
Demand for labour	Incomes and spending power – aggregate demand. Shifting patterns of consumer demand led by fashions, tastes or new product development. Economic cycles – recessions reduce demand for labour. The price of capital equipment. If it falls, employers will substitute capital for labour and vice versa. Technological change.

Human capital

Economic cycles

The demand for labour is a **derived demand**: it depends upon the demand for individual products. Employers take on more people when their products are selling well. **Wage rates** will depend on the interaction of supply and demand.

Often the available labour is not in the place where it is most needed. Structural change means that some areas find that demand for their traditional products is falling. These areas will suffer from unemployment (in industrial areas) and from underemployment (in agricultural areas). There will be an excess supply of labour.

Obsolete skills

Where structural changes are under way, skilled people may find that their particular skills are obsolete. It may take a long time for them to find new jobs. When they do find work, it may be less well paid and involve moving to a different region. Developments in technology and trading arrangements very often disrupt employment. An excess supply of labour may develop.

| Excess supply of labour | Rising unemployment | More long-term unemployed | Need to acquire new skills | Or go where labour is in demand |

Occupational and geographical immobility

Rising unemployment in specific sectors is easier to deal with if the people affected are occupationally or geographically mobile. Transferable skills also help. **Flexible labour markets** exist where people are capable of adapting to changing patterns of demand. If they are multi-skilled they may have few problems with change – they are already a part of the flexible labour market.

> **Flexible labour markets** exist where employers can take on new employees on a full-time or part-time basis, temporarily or permanently, at wage levels determined by market rates, and can make people redundant when they need to and without great expense.

The importance of skills, training and education

Rising demand for particular products will induce employers to recruit more people. If there is unemployment there may be no problem. But very often recruiting skilled people takes time. There will be excess demand for some groups within the labour force.

| Skill shortages | Excess demand for scarce skills | Wages rise | More people get trained | But training takes time |

Unskilled people find that they are disadvantaged. They will be expecting reasonable pay but potential employers may be offshoring production to economies where wage rates are lower. Many unskilled people are competing in this way with people in emerging economies. In order to find work they have to get as much training as they can.

Transferable skills

Training increases productivity and makes people more employable. Multi-skilling makes employees more flexible – if they are not needed for one job, they can do a different one. This in turn helps businesses to adapt to changing circumstances. Transferable skills work similarly – skilled people can sometimes find a similar job in a different business. Electricians may be able to work in a different industry. In general skilled people earn very much more than the unskilled.

Productivity

Where there is excess demand for people with particular qualifications, skill shortages will hamper growth. Economic growth requires rising productivity, people who can find new ways of doing things and cost effective approaches to production. These trends rely on the availability of skilled people.

Global competition, recession and redundancies

Global competition is visible in a range of very different markets. Global competition can push up wages and prices where scarce resources and scarce skills present problems.

● There is competition in the global labour market to recruit the best people for the job.

● Many UK businesses report difficulty in getting highly qualified people and the importance of being able to recruit people from abroad in order to get the best and most productive. This is a particular issue in relation to Brexit, which will involve strict control of migration.

● There is competition to produce the cheapest products, or at least the best value for money. This affects businesses that cannot innovate fast enough to stay competitive with the best.

● There is competition to get access to scarce resources, in particular mineral resources. Some governments try hard to ensure access. Chinese FDI in Africa is designed to ensure ready access to scarce minerals.

Recession

Recession reduces the demand for labour. You can see this very clearly in Figure 1. In the recession that followed the financial crisis of 2008-9, unemployment rose sharply and pay was greatly affected. Many people in the UK accepted pay cuts rather than lose their jobs.

Figure 1: UK unemployment

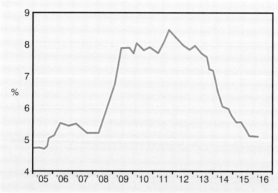

Source: ONS

Redundancies

Figure 2: Redundancies in the UK 1996-2016

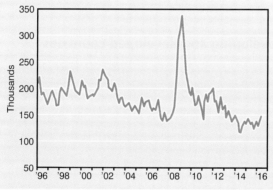

Source: ONS

Recession creates unemployment for all except the people with the scarcest skills. People with obsolete or no skills, seeking work, will have the most difficulty finding employment.

Redundancies occur most often in recessions, but can occur any time. You can see the scale of redundancies in the 2008-12 recession in Figure 2.

> **Think!**
> Why are redundancies usually well over 100,000 a year even when the economy is growing?

● Whenever a business finds itself unable to compete, there is a significant possibility of redundancy.

Cutting costs

● The business can close down OR cut production costs. Closing down may cause all employees to be made redundant.

● Cutting production costs may involve either new equipment – capital investment – or new ways of working e.g. lean production.

● Sometimes this can be achieved simply by retraining existing employees and not recruiting any new ones for a while, so that numbers employed fall gradually by natural wastage.

● Trade union members with few or no skills may have a high risk of redundancy.

Impact of trade unions and professional bodies

Protecting individual employees

● The purpose of trade unions is to act on behalf of the members to safeguard their interests by negotiating pay and ensuring good working conditions.

● Trade unions are important for people who work for big powerful companies that can cut costs by saving on pay and conditions. By having a single representative, the members can rely on skilled union negotiators that are themselves powerful enough to protect them.

● Professional bodies work in the same way to protect members. (The British Medical Association can call on people with excellent negotiating skills to protect doctors' pay within the UK NHS.) Unlike trade unions, professional bodies can restrict the number of people joining the profession.

● In developed economies, employees are often protected by the law and regulation. So many fewer people join trade unions nowadays. In the past, and in emerging economies now, trade unions were and are vital; they can help to prevent seriously unethical business behaviour including exploitation of labour and dangerous working conditions. (Exploitation of labour means paying less than the value of the work done.)

Bargaining power

● Where unions and professional bodies are able to push pay above a certain level, they can constrain competitiveness. In time, the business may close down. Similarly, efforts to oppose the introduction of new equipment and new ways of working can prevent an increase in efficiency that might make the business more competitive, more profitable and capable of offering higher pay.

3.5.3 Minimum wage legislation

To prevent very low pay and protect employees who have little or no bargaining power, minimum wages can ensure that pay does not fall below reasonable limits. All employers are required by law to pay at least the amount of the minimum wage. Unless enforcement is active, they may simply ignore it.

Minimum wages in developing and developed countries

Example
The USA has had a federal minimum wage since 1933. It is currently US$7.25 per hour though some states have higher rates. San Francisco will be the first to set the rate at $15 in 2018. US congress researchers estimated that raising the federal rate to $10.10 (£9 at today's exchange rate) in 2016 would increase the wages of 16.5 million people in the US.

Addressing low pay

A minimum wage rate was introduced in the UK in 1999, at £3.60 per hour. It had risen to £7.20 an hour by 2016. It is set to rise to £9 per hour by 2020. Altogether 190 economies have minimum wage rates but most are very low. They have the potential to raise incomes and consumer spending power and reduce poverty.

Q Why do we need minimum wages?

These minimum wages are about providing the absolute minimum needed to survive. In a global labour market, people in developed economies need some protection from the competition in emerging economies, where most prices are lower than they are in developed economies. In developing and emerging economies minimum wages are rarely high enough to reduce employment or to affect competitiveness.

Q Why have minimum wages been kept so low?

Avoiding redundancies

Economic theory suggests that if wages rise, employers will recruit fewer people. They will look for ways to reduce their need for labour and go for capital intensive production. However many economists have argued that with minimum wages as low as they are, they are unlikely to have a significant effect on employment levels. UK unemployment did not rise after 1999. But we do not know what will happen when the increases proposed by Chancellor Osborne in 2015 are implemented. This might make more of a

Evidence suggests that when employers have to pay a bit more, they make more effort to train their employees and raise their productivity.

difference. However, most unemployment can be traced to structural change, labour immobilities or recession.

Q Will higher minimum wages lead to reduced competitiveness?

Changes in minimum wage rates in the UK have not so far reduced job availability or had any noticeable effect on export prices. The evidence suggests that when employers have to pay a bit more, they make more effort to train their employees and raise their productivity. The New Living Wage may or may not be high enough to induce some employers to manage with a smaller labour force.

Skill shortages and their impact on international competitiveness

Skill shortages are sometimes so widespread that they affect many economies. There is a global shortage of engineers. The wage differential between those with and those without qualifications is large.

- Germany has always prioritised skills training and engineering courses. It is one of the world's most successful exporters of high quality machinery and other sophisticated manufactures.

- The UK has had serious skill shortages for a long time. As of 2016, there is a new apprenticeship scheme. It will force large and medium sized businesses to do much more training instead of looking to poach skilled people from competing businesses. The UK business world is furious but PM May says the scheme will go ahead anyway.

- Structural change – the development of new industries and types of business – increases demand for certain types of skills. Education and training take time and effort. You cannot suddenly create more engineers. Business needs for scarce skills develop faster than training facilities.

- People with scarce skills can earn more. This does affect competitiveness. Quality training programmes benefit the whole economy. Their absence can restrict growth.

Migration

Migration is part of the human experience. Growing populations need more space. But now, falling birth rates have made migration highly significant. Migrants can help to provide scarce skills and stimulate economic growth.

Striving for competitiveness

Example

Japan has a falling population. In time other economies will face a shortage of younger people to look after their ageing populations as well as doing skilled work. But many in the ageing populations do not want migrants. Where birth rates are falling and migrants are excluded, economic growth will decline and perhaps go into reverse. Japan has few immigrants and is struggling to achieve continuing economic growth.

Migration within economies is about moving from a place where there are few jobs on offer to a place where there are many jobs on offer.

Geographical mobility

● Scots and Welsh may move to south-east England. If they have scarce skills they may be able to afford the high cost of housing. If not they may stay in areas of high unemployment. House price differentials account for higher unemployment rates outside south-east England.

● Mass migration has occurred in China as people moved from farming communities to areas where manufacturing has developed. The same is happening now in India and many other emerging economies.

Migration between economies occurs when people move to another country in search of work. When job vacancies are rising and skill shortages are a real problem, recruiting migrants helps to keep the economy growing.

Migrants keep prices down

● Migrants from Mexico and other Latin American economies (sometimes not legal) provide cheap labour for US farming communities.

● If this source of labour is cut off under the Trump presidency, US farms will face labour shortages and will have to pay higher wages to recruit local farm workers.

● Food prices will rise. People on low incomes will face increasing poverty. The better off will have less to spend on non-food products.

● Falling demand for non-food products will hurt businesses selling non-food goods and services. The same arguments apply to the UK.

Inequality and incentives

Inequality can be caused in three ways, by:

● very low wage rates. In developed economies, people on very low pay may have no incentive to work if benefit levels are near to or higher than wage rates for unskilled work – they are in a poverty trap. (See pages 54-5.) Wage rates may be below the level needed to maintain health and wellbeing.

● very high incomes that are not heavily taxed.

● accumulated wealth – when some people own or buy valuable assets that give them unearned income (dividends, rent and interest).

People who are in the poverty trap can be helped in two ways:

● Minimum wages may raise their pay sufficiently to create an incentive to work.

Tax credits

● **Working Tax Credits** ensure that everyone is better off in work than unemployed. Tax credits were introduced in 1999.

> **Working tax credits** in the UK are designed so that everyone who is available for work is better off working than not.

Example

During the recession, 2008-12, unemployment did not increase nearly so much as it had in previous recessions. Many employers reduced working hours and cut pay, so many employed people would have fallen into the poverty trap. That they kept working suggests that tax credits do create a real incentive.

Chapter 6

Inequality and re-distribution

Terms to revise: Human Development Index (HDI) Revision Guide Theme 2 page 88.

Poverty and inequality

Global inequality

> **A report by the OECD in December 2014 made these points...**
> - Inequality across the world is rising fast and has increased in both low and high income economies alike.
> - The gap between rich and poor is at its highest level in most OECD countries in 30 years.
> - The richest 10% of the population in the OECD area earn 9.5 times more than the poorest 10%.
> - By contrast, in the 1980s the ratio stood at 7:1.
> - This long-term trend increase in income inequality has curbed economic growth significantly.

Absolute and relative poverty

- Poverty is a term used widely but can be hard to define accurately, which is why we use measures of poverty to identify trends and make comparisons.

- Absolute poverty is a straightforward term and means the lack of one or more basic needs over a period long enough that it endangers your life or can cause it harm. These needs include food, water, clothing and shelter.

- Relative poverty becomes more difficult to define; it depends on where you are. Relative poverty in the UK is not the same as it is for a slum dweller in a developing country.

> **Relative poverty** applies to people who do not have enough income to participate fully in the society in which they live. It will vary according to the standard of living at the time.
>
> **Absolute poverty** means not having enough income to provide the basic necessities and survive.

Measures of poverty: national measures

UK poverty

- The UK government and the EU define the poverty line more precisely as 60 per cent of the median UK household income, after housing costs have been paid. Households receiving less than this are classified as poor. This amounts to £250 a week or less at the moment.

> **Relative poverty in the UK (2013 figures)**
> - 13½ million people in the UK were living in households below this low-income threshold. This is around 1 in 5 of the population.
> - 3.5 million children were living in poverty (after housing costs).
> - The UK has **proportionally more** children in poverty than most rich countries.
> - The UK has a higher proportion of its population on relative low incomes than most other EU countries.
> - The Joseph Rowntree Foundation estimates that child poverty costs £25 billion each year in costs to the Exchequer and reduced GDP.

International measures

- The World Bank measures extreme poverty as all those living on US$1.25 a day or less. In 2015 that included 1 billion people.

International poverty

- Another common measurement of poverty in developing countries includes all those living on $2 or less per day; that total is 2.2 billion.

- An attempt to look beyond a narrow income measure is the Global Multidimensional Poverty Index or MPI. This brings together 10 indicators including safe water, sanitation, child mortality, education and health.

- The MPI of 2014 found a total of 1.6 billion people living in multidimensional poverty. Of these 1.6 billion people, 52% live in South Asia (mainly the Indian sub-continent), and 29% in Sub-Saharan Africa.

Measures of inequality

Gini coefficient

The **Gini coefficient** is a numerical representation of inequality calculated from the Lorenz Curve.

In the diagrams below the Gini Coefficient = Area A/(Area A + Area B).

The answer will be between 0 (complete equality) and 1 (complete inequality).

> The **Gini coefficient** provides an objective measure of income inequality and can range from 0 to 1. A coefficient of 0 would mean income is shared equally between all individuals, whilst a coefficient of 1 would mean one person within the population has all the income and everyone else none. The higher the Gini coefficient figure, the higher the level of inequality.

Sweden's Gini coefficient is .25 – inequality is below that of most other nations. Inequality tends to be highest in the Americas – mostly between .4 and 5. Other Gini coefficients are .42 for China, .36 for the UK, and .41 for the USA.

Lorenz curve

The Lorenz curve is a diagram that shows inequality within an economy.

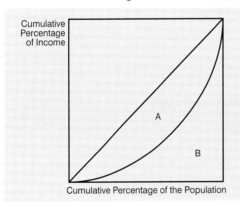
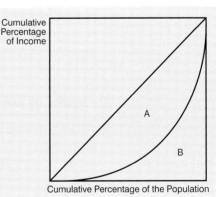

The axes of the diagram are cumulative percentages increasing from the origin. The horizontal axis shows percentages of the population. The vertical axis shows percentages of income.

The straight diagonal line at 45 degrees represents complete equality, 30% of the population have 30% of the income, 90% of the population have 90% of the income. *The curved line is the Lorenz Curve. The further that bows out from the diagonal, the greater the level of inequality.*

3.6.2 Reducing poverty

Economic development and economic growth are not the same.

Per capita income

- **Economic growth** means the rate of growth of GDP. If the population is growing faster than the economy, per capita income may be falling. Many economies are growing fast but still have a high percentage of their population living in poverty.

Economic development

- **Economic development** refers not just to the growth of incomes but also to the quality of life. You explored this when studying the HDI, which measures improvements in health and education as well as incomes.

When emerging economies grow very fast, incomes improve and this does reduce poverty levels. However, it may take much longer to set up the institutions that can foster a deeper level of development.

- Schools may improve slowly due to lack of well-trained teachers and money for educational resources. Health care may be fragile because there are too few doctors and hospitals.

- Governments may not provide welfare benefits.

- Problems can be solved by collecting taxes and spending wisely but the enforcement of tax collection may be weak. It may be impossible to reduce tax evasion quickly and corruption may make matters worse.

Example
In emerging economies, governments often have difficulty in ensuring that their tax revenue is well spent. Corrupt construction companies that are building schools have been known to use cheaper materials than the government regulations specified. If the buildings are destroyed by earthquakes or floods, because of their poor structure, little has been achieved.

International aid, welfare, and NGOs

Aid comes in two forms: bilateral and multilateral.

Multilateral aid

- Bilateral aid is provided by individual developed country governments to individual developing or emerging country governments. Multilateral aid is distributed by international organisations, primarily the World Bank and the UN.

NGOs

- Non-governmental organisations (NGOs) provide all kinds of support, often directly targeted to improve welfare in a range of ways. They are usually charities that get donations from the public.

International organisations, government and NGOs can all help by:

- Funding infrastructure development.

- Improving welfare such as anti-malaria kit (e.g. The Gates Foundation) or emergency medical care (Médecins sans Frontières i.e. Doctors Without Borders).

- Sending whatever is needed when major natural disasters threaten many people.

- Supporting communities in poor and war-torn regions.

Poverty reduction policies – in developing and emerging economies:

Providing aid is controversial. Many people have pointed out that free trade, giving access to large markets in the developed economies, is of more use to developing and emerging economies than aid donations. This is why trade agreements matter. But some aid does work, if it is appropriate to the needs of the destination country.

Foreign aid

- Some people are unconcerned about poverty in other, poorer countries and request their governments to 'take care of your own'. They do not identify with disadvantaged people whom they perceive as 'different'.

- Some aid has been wasted. Governments are particularly likely to give aid for projects that suit themselves, e.g. by sending their own exports. Governments and NGOs set up aid projects that are inappropriate to the needs of the economy concerned.

- Some aid money goes into the pockets of corrupt officials. But some aid works really well to help people and to speed up the development process.

Aid helps

● Aid can provide some economies with technical know-how that helps to make production more efficient and exports more competitive.

● Aid saves lives when there are disasters, helps to provide clean water and access to electricity.

● Investment in infrastructure, health care and education does help to foster economic growth in the long run, even though it takes time.

● Over time, as incomes rise and governments work to collect taxes, welfare provision can be introduced to protect vulnerable people.

This is very worthwhile because poverty tends to persist if not tackled.

| Growing up in a poor family | *often* | means being poorly educated and getting few qualifications | *so that* | only poorly paid jobs are accessible | *and* | the next generation will have a similar story to tell |

...and in developed economies

● Income redistribution helps. (See pages 54-5.)

● Building homes reduces the cost of housing. (Much UK poverty is caused by the high cost of housing at the present time.)

Welfare benefits

● Benefits keep many people from the worst effects of poverty.

● Making sure that everyone has an incentive to find a job, e.g. through tax credits.

● Governments should try to avoid false economies – e.g. make sure that community care works for people leaving hospital so that they do not have to occupy an expensive hospital bed.

3.6.3 The impact of inequality on economic agents

Inequality and individuals

Poverty has wide-ranging and at times, devastating, social and economic impacts. For those individuals who are affected, the quality of life is poor; there is hardship and suffering on a personal level. But the costs go far beyond the individual.

● Research findings often link social problems common in developed societies to problems originating in poverty. These include reduced life expectancy, child mortality, drugs, crime, homicide rates, mental illness and obesity.

Costs of poverty

● Many of these problems associated with inequality are expensive to deal with and so they have a high opportunity cost; money spent on policing and social services could be spent on education or infrastructure improvements.

● According to the Child Poverty Action Group (CPAG) in 2013 the high levels of child poverty in the UK are currently costing at least £29 billion a year – or £1,098 per household.

Costs to individuals and families	Costs to society
● Poor quality **housing**, possible homelessness.	● Loss of **output**, where unemployment is the problem.
● Increased **illness**, lower life expectancy, mental health problems.	● Direct costs: **benefits** and public services.
● Limited access to good quality **education** and training.	● **Social problems** such as teenage pregnancy, crime and vandalism.
● A sense of being trapped in a **hopeless** situation that saps motivation to work.	● Despair that leads to **health problems** that have no cheap solution.

**Low
disposable
incomes**

Impact of inequality and poverty on business and the economy

● People with low levels of income clearly spend less; growing inequality and poverty alters the pattern of demand for goods and services.

● Mainstream businesses may suffer but those targeting the poor and the rich may thrive.

● Low wages at the bottom end of the income range may be attractive to some businesses that want to reduce costs or who have labour intensive production.

● Low levels of education and training may deter businesses from investing or locating where this is a problem.

● Social costs can be higher and divert resources from elsewhere.

● Political instability caused by increasing poverty and resentment of the wealthy can create business uncertainty.

On firms: connections between low income and low productivity

Economists have long thought that there is a link between income and productivity. Low-income workers tend to lack educational attainment and feel less involved. As a result they are likely to be both less capable and a likely constraint on productivity growth.

Research indicates that higher pay has the following impacts...

**Raising
pay means:**

● Workers are more motivated.

● More able and productive workers are attracted.

● There is less turnover, reducing costs of hiring and training.

● There is less absenteeism.

● Quality and customer service improve.

● Less need for direct supervision.

● Workers have better health which reinforces the above points.

Low-income workers tend to lack educational attainment and feel less involved.

On the economy

● At the end of 2014 the OECD published a report on the impact of income inequality. It found that economies where income inequality is decreasing grow faster than those with rising inequality.

● Rising inequality is estimated to have knocked more than 10 percentage points off growth in Mexico and New Zealand between 1988 and 2008.

● In Italy, the United Kingdom and the United States, the cumulative growth rate would have been six to nine percentage points higher had income inequality not increased.

Redistribution

● By contrast, greater equality helped increase GDP per capita in Spain, France and Ireland prior to the financial crisis.

● The most direct policy tool to reduce inequality is redistribution through taxes and benefits

● Rich people save more than poor people do. Higher savings mean reduced aggregate demand. (Savings are a leakage from the circular flow of money, see RG Theme 2, page 97.)

● Inequality can destabilise the economy if political unrest creates uncertainty.

3.6.4 Re-distribution of income and wealth

- A certain amount of redistribution happens on a global scale through foreign aid (see pages 51-2). It helps to re-distribute income and wealth, but only to a limited extent and only when it is working as it should do.

- FDI can help too – by creating employment in emerging and developing economies.

- In the developed economies income is re-distributed through tax and benefit policies.

- In emerging economies it may be difficult to do this if tax collection is poorly enforced.

The distinction between income and wealth

In economics, wealth and income mean different things. Both, when growing, can increase inequality.

Income tax

> **Income** is the payment made in return for labour and is seen as a *flow* over a period of time, for example a teacher's income might be £32,000 a year.
>
> **Wealth** is a *stock* and is the monetary value placed on the assets a person owns at a specific moment in time. Wealth might include property, savings, investments, cars and so on.

Income tax reduces incomes above the personal allowance. Wealth itself is generally not taxed in the UK (except by stamp duties on the sale of homes and inheritance taxes) but the income derived from it will be taxed (dividends, interest and rent). These are the taxes that help to redistribute income. The revenue can be used to provide benefits.

Incentives and the poverty trap

> The **poverty trap** describes the situation when someone would be even poorer or not much richer if they had a job, because they would no longer receive financial help from the government. They will have little or no incentive to seek employment.

- Finding work may mean losing benefits and paying more tax, which may mean that net income stays the same or increases very little, or actually falls.

Disincentives

- This can be a real disincentive to finding a job.

- Critics argue that this wastes taxpayers' money and that too many people take advantage of benefits and make little effort to find work.

- It is a tricky situation: there is a trade-off, between reducing expenditure and increasing employment, and the importance of avoiding unfair treatment of the low paid, especially those with children.

- There is an additional issue because paying inadequate benefits to families may worsen some social problems with long term consequences for society.

Tax credits

- The solution to this problem in the UK is tax credits (see page 48). They provide an incentive to work. They appear to have the desired effect. Many long term unemployed have found work since they were introduced in 1999.

The poverty trap describes the situation when someone would be poorer or not much richer if they had a job.

New Living Wage

Example

Chancellor Osborne tried suggesting cuts to tax credits in 2015 because the costs had grown. There was a major public outcry. In the event, he did cut tax credits but by rather less than the amount originally proposed. His introduction of the New Living Wage should help to reduce the cost of tax credits as well as raising low incomes.

Policies to reduce the poverty trap	Problems with specific policies
Reducing benefits would increase the incentive to work.	Increases inequality and causes genuine hardship to those who want to work when unemployment is high and few jobs are available.
Increasing the Income Tax threshold would mean that more money can be earned before tax has to be paid.	Reduces the government's tax revenue as it applies to all workers. Reduction in benefits may be less than the tax loss.
Increasing the minimum wage rates would create a bigger incentive to work.	If set too high it may cause a rise in unemployment. For employers, costs would increase. May reduce competitiveness.
Making it harder to get sickness and disability benefits may make work more attractive.	Some people may genuinely need these payments.
Capping the maximum benefits paid may increase incentives.	May push large families into real hardship.
Using tax credits that make everyone better off working.	Can become expensive if employers are paying very low wages.

Incentives

Taxation and the provision of services

The Budget

Each year the government sets out its fiscal policy in the budget statements. These indicate how the government will raise revenue via taxation and how it will subsequently spend it.

There are two main types of taxation...

Direct taxation – including Income tax, National Insurance and corporation tax – direct taxes are charged on earnings.

Indirect taxation include VAT, excise duties (e.g. on petrol and alcohol), car tax, insurance tax and others.

Taxation has several functions:

● It allows the government to provide a wide range of services that it considers necessary for the benefit of the country; these include healthcare, education and benefits that are especially helpful to people living in poverty.

● It re-distributes income by transferring money from those that have it to those that need it such as the unemployed, disabled and pensioners.

● Income tax redistributes income if it is progressive so that richer people pay more tax than poorer people. The richest pay higher rate income tax at 40%, or 45% if they earn over £150,000.

Theme 3 – Glossary

Some relevant terms for Theme 3 are in the glossaries for the Revision Guide for Themes 1 and 2.

Absolute poverty is not having enough income to provide the basic necessities for survival.

Aid is given by both governments and NGOs to countries that are struggling to reduce poverty or deal with disasters.

Balance of payments: the accounts that record all international transactions, including trade and capital movements.

BRIC stands for Brazil, Russia, India and China, four of the world's largest growing economies.

Commodities are raw materials or semi-manufactured products that are traded in bulk and are not recognisably originating from any particular business. Examples include iron ore, cotton, wheat and oil.

Common markets have completely free trade internally and a single unified trade policy covering all member countries' trade with the rest of the world.

Corporate culture is the set of important assumptions that are shared by people working in a particular business and influence the ways in which decisions are taken there.

Corporate social responsibility means taking decisions that reflect all stakeholders' interests.

Current account of the balance of payments records all trade in goods and services.

Developed countries include most of Europe, Japan, the USA, Canada and Australia. All have high incomes. Through capital investment, they have acquired sophisticated production facilities.

Developing countries have relatively low standards of living, compared to developed countries. They may have small manufacturing sectors; many people may be engaged in agriculture.

Diversifying means selling more than one product, or the same product in more than one market. If one market shrinks, profits can still be made with other products or in other markets.

Economic growth refers to the rate of growth of output, real incomes and GDP.

Emerging economies are characterised by rapid economic growth. They have seen big increases in manufacturing output and standards of living are rising. Some would still be described as poor countries (e.g. India) but others (e.g. Mexico) are well on the way to becoming developed countries.

Ethical decision making means following codes of practice that embody moral values. The objective is to do the right thing, acting with honesty and integrity.

Ethnocentric Model: an approach to marketing based on the tendency to look at the world primarily from the perspective of one's own culture. A business may simply do the same everywhere as it does in its home market.

The European Union (EU) is a trade bloc that has become a single market.

Eurozone refers to the 19 EU members that use the euro as a single currency.

Free trade areas are groups of countries that trade completely freely with each other, with no trade barriers, but each member country retains its own independent trade policies in relation to the rest of the world.

Geocentric approach sees the world as a potential market with both similarities and differences in domestic and foreign markets. An effort is made to develop integrated world market strategies to gain the best from both of these strands.

The **Gini coefficient** provides an objective measure of income inequality and can range from 0 to 1. A coefficient of 0 would mean income is shared equally between all individuals, whilst a coefficient of 1 would mean one person within the population has all the income and everyone else none.

Global market niches are smaller, more specialised parts of a global market where customers in more than one country have particular needs that are not fully met by the global mass market.

Glocalisation combines the words 'globalisation' and 'localisation' to emphasise the idea that a global product or service is more likely to succeed if it is adapted to the specific requirements of local practices and cultural expectations.

The **Human Development Index** is constructed by the United Nations Development Program and provides a measure of development based on access to health care and education as well as national income. It therefore includes qualitative as well as quantitative aspects of development.

Incentives are financial rewards that can influence decisions. Individuals may respond to an incentive to work. Businesses may respond to incentives to invest (e.g. lower interest rates).

Index numbers can be created for any time series data so that comparisons can be made more easily.

The **IMF**, International Monetary Fund, co-ordinates the international monetary system. It tries to keep the system stable, providing adequate finance for world trade to continue uninterrupted.

Inequality refers to big differences in incomes and wealth within societies. China, the USA and Latin American countries have the most unequal distributions of income and wealth; the UK has greater inequality than most other European countries, but this may change.

Interdependence refers to the way in which different economies have become increasingly reliant on one another through trade, capital movements and international agreements.

Lorenz Curve shows the extent of inequality in a particular economy. It plots the percentage of the population that receives each decile (e.g. 10% or 20%) of total income.

Market saturation occurs when it becomes impossible to expand sales further in that particular market.

Migration occurs when people move from one region to another or from one country to another, seeking employment (or sometimes, just safety).

Minimum wage is the minimum rate of pay per hour that must by law be paid by employers.

Nominal value means value in money terms at current prices. No allowance is made for inflation.

Non-governmental organisations (**NGOs**): a term applied to not-for-profit organisations that either act as pressure groups or as charities or both.

Non-price competition refers to any competitive activity that does not involve cutting prices.

Offshoring means locating production in a foreign country. The objective may be to exploit cost savings, most often lower wage rates. Or it may be to be close to a thriving market or to avoid trade barriers.

Polycentric Model: an approach that considers each target market to be unique. Each of its subsidiary businesses develop unique business and marketing strategies that suit the relevant location.

The **poverty trap** is a situation in which someone would be even poorer or not much richer if they had a job because they would no longer receive unemployment benefits from the government.

Protectionism is any government policy aimed at protecting the domestic economy from competing imports. Trade barriers can protect specific domestic industries and their employees by raising the prices of imported products. They will benefit but not the consumers whose purchasing power is reduced by high prices.

Pressure groups are organisations that attempt to influence public policy and especially government legislation, regarding their particular concerns and priorities.

Professional bodies represent groups of professionally qualified people in specific types of work. Examples include the BMA, the Law Society and the Institute of Chartered Accountants.

Purchasing Power Parity (**PPP**) is a way of adjusting monetary values to allow for differences in prices between countries.

Quotas are physical limits on the level of specific imports in any one year.

Rationalisation means closing down parts of a firm that duplicate some functions. It may happen after a merger, e.g. when one bank merges with another, any one branch that is close to another in the same group will be kept open while any others are closed down.

Real values can be calculated to show changes in values with the effects of inflation removed. In other words, all values are expressed at constant prices.

Redundancies are job losses that result from fewer employees being needed, because of rationalisation, using more capital intensive production or falling demand for the product.

Relative poverty affects people who do not have enough income to participate in the normal life of the society in which they live.

Risks are threats that may or may not occur, but can be quantified using probabilities.

Social and cultural differences: individual societies and groups may have a distinctive way of life, affecting their choice of product. This will also affect the way they do business with one another.

Subcultures are groups of people who have interests and values in common. They may be based on hobbies, life-styles, ethnic or religious background or just personal enthusiasms and preferences. Businesses may target subcultures as potentially profitable niche markets.

Subsidies are sums of money paid by the government to a producer, so that the price to the customer will be lower than it otherwise would have been. Within the EU, most subsidies actually go to farmers, so that some food prices are lower than the cost of production.

Supply chains are sequences of processes that follow one another from start to finish of production.

Tariffs are taxes on imported goods. They make the price higher; sales will generally be lower.

Technology and skills transfer occurs when FDI brings new businesses into an economy and employees learn new skills that they take with them when they change jobs.

Trade blocs are groups of countries where barriers to trade are reduced or eliminated between member states.

Trade creation occurs when there is an increase in the total amount of goods and services traded because of reduced trade restrictions within a trading bloc.

Trade diversion occurs when a trading bloc reduces imports from non-member countries, enabling businesses within member countries to increase sales inside the trading bloc.

Trade liberalisation refers to the process of reducing barriers to trade so that economies can move gradually closer to free trade, which would ultimately mean that there are no trade barriers at all.

Trade unions are organisations that represent employees in negotiations with employers.

Transfer pricing occurs when one part of an MNC in one country transfers (sells) goods or services to another part in another country. The price charged is the 'transfer price'. This may be unrelated to costs incurred and can be set at a level which reduces profit and hence the total tax paid.

Wealth consists of accumulated assets, including bank deposits, shares, property and businesses.

Working conditions refer to possible events in workplaces that may affect the welfare of employees.

The **World Bank** (proper name International Bank for Reconstruction and Development) lends to developing countries in order to fund projects which will help them to raise incomes and make their economies more efficient.

The **WTO**, World Trade Organisation, started out as GATT, the General Agreement on Tariffs and Trade. It supervises world trading arrangements and trade negotiations and helps to resolve disputes between governments and businesses.

Terms to revise: pricing strategies, (Revision Guide, Theme 2, pages 71-2), non-price competition, (RG, Theme 2, pages 73-4), product and process innovation, (RG Theme 2, pages 62-3), allocation of resources, (RG Theme 1, pages 1 & 39), product differentiation, (RG Theme 1, pages 29-31), economies of scale, (RG Theme 2, pages 57-9), average, fixed and variable costs, (RG Theme 1, page 45), contribution, (RG Theme 1, pages 46-7), lean production, (RG Theme 2, pages 79-82), market orientation, (RG Theme 1, page 31).

Market structure is all about how many businesses there are competing in the market, and how they behave in relation to one another. This involves looking at a whole range of factors:

Market structure

- The number of businesses in the market.
- The amount and type of competition.
- The nature of the product.
- The degree of power each business has.
- The degree of power that consumers have.
- The extent to which the business can influence price or output.
- Profit levels.
- How businesses behave – pricing strategies and types of non-price competition.
- The extent of barriers to entry and exit.
- The impact on efficiency.

From this we can place businesses in different categories or types of market and then place them along a spectrum.

The spectrum of competition

Market structures fall into categories, which can be shown on a diagram of the **spectrum of competition**. It has **perfect competition** at one end and **pure monopoly** at the other. These are extreme situations and real world businesses are all located in the space between them.

Perfect competition

- The closer a market is towards monopoly, the more it takes on the characteristics of a monopoly and the less competitive it becomes.

- The closer a market is towards perfect competition the more competitive it becomes and the closer it gets to the characteristics of perfect competition.

Pure monopoly

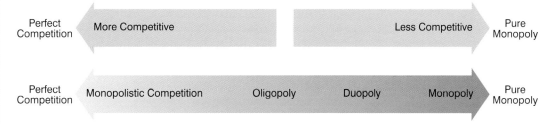

Monopoly

A monopoly occurs when there is only one business operating in the market. The **pure monopoly**, with only one firm in the market and no competition, is very rare. However, in practical terms, one firm may well dominate an industry and possess a large amount of **monopoly power**.

A **legal monopoly** exists when a firm has 25% or more of its market. This means that the Competition and Markets Authority (CMA) can intervene in the market if the business is thought to be acting against the public interest. (The CMA is a government body that exists to ensure that businesses comply with competition law.)

Natural monopolies

A **natural monopoly** may exist when it would be wasteful to have more than one business providing a service e.g. a rail network or water supply. (Natural monopolies have regulators, government bodies set up to ensure that they do not exploit the customer.)

Monopoly markets have the following characteristics:

● Monopolies have the ability to set either price or output levels

● Prices tend to be higher with a monopoly

● There are considerable barriers to entry

● Consumer choice may be severely restricted

● Profits will be higher than they would be in a competitive situation.

> **Monopoly power** is the ability to affect price levels; either to charge higher prices, or to lower them in order to take market share away from smaller rivals. It refers to the ability to restrict output, to affect outcomes in the market and dictate what happens.
>
> **Duopoly** – occurs where two large firms dominate the market e.g. Visa and Mastercard.

Oligopoly

In an oligopoly, several large firms dominate the market and compete with each other. Supermarkets, petrol companies and high street banks are all examples of this.

● An oligopoly may have considerable monopoly power.

Non-price competition

● Oligopolies are often characterised by non-price competition such as heavy branding and promotion.

● Competing on price is usually avoided as a price war can be damaging to profits.

● Although a few large firms dominate the market, there are likely to be many smaller firms, often in niche markets. For example, the brewing industry is dominated by huge multinational companies such as Anheuser Busch, yet small local breweries continue to thrive.

● With an oligopoly, there is always a danger of collusion (illegally reaching an agreement to fix prices or control output at the expense of the consumer).

● There are high barriers to entry.

● Abnormal profits will be made.

> An **oligopoly** is said to exist when the concentration ratio shows that a specific number of firms (say, five) in the market account for more than 60% of that market.

Oligopolies may indulge in predatory pricing. They may try to undercut competitors that have higher costs than they do, charging prices at which the competitor cannot survive.

Imperfect competition

Imperfect competition is an umbrella term that covers all those situations where competition exists but is not as strong as it might be. There will be distortions in the market that prevent it from being fully competitive. It includes oligopoly and also **monopolistic competition**.

Monopolistic competition

Monopolistic competition occurs where there are many firms in the market, each offering a slightly differentiated product and all competing with each other. Your hairdresser may be a good example. It will not be the same as all other hairdressers – each has individual features. But they certainly do compete. Other examples include estate agents and craft beer producers.

- There are many firms producing similar, but not identical products and there is product differentiation.

- There are many producers and many consumers in the market and they act independently.

- Consumers are aware of both price and non-price differences among the competitors' products.

Barriers to entry and exit

- The barriers to entry and exit, into and out of the market, are relatively low or sometimes non-existent. For example, small shops can rent premises and get started very easily.

- Producers have some control over prices.

> ### ⚠ WATCH OUT!
>
> Do not confuse **Monopolistic** behaviour with a monopoly.
>
> They are easily confused, **never use monopolistic to describe any kind of monopoly behaviour**. 'Monopolistic' just means that businesses have an element of market power, and this may be quite small.

Using the model of perfect competition to explain how markets work

Perfect competition is a theoretical idea; it is a model that defines the greatest possible degree of competition. It implies a market with countless buyers and sellers and identical products. In reality it almost never exists but currency trading and some commodity products come close. The following conditions must be there for it to exist.

Homogeneous products

- The product is homogeneous, meaning exactly the same so that it is impossible to tell the difference between products from different suppliers.

- There are many buyers and many sellers, none of which are big enough to influence price.

- Firms have no control over price; all are **price takers**.

- There are no barriers to entry or exit.

Perfect knowledge

- There is perfect knowledge, consumers and suppliers know about everything that happens, as it happens and have full information on all aspects of the market, including new technologies.

- Only **normal profit** is made.

> **Normal profit** is the amount of profit required for the firm to stay in business. Any less and it will be unable to cover all of its costs.
>
> **Price takers** cannot choose the prices they charge – they must sell at the price prevailing in the marketplace because of the strong competition.

- Perfect competition provides us with a useful model and a guide as to how a competitive market works where there are no imperfections at all.

- Markets bring together potential buyers and sellers; if all have perfect knowledge then the sellers will know what the buyers want and respond by producing it.

- With so many producers there will be intense competition and any producer that is not competitive on price will not sell; all resources must be used efficiently.

- An increase in demand will lead to more firms entering the market: there are no barriers to

Normal profit is the amount of profit required for the firm to stay in business.

entry. In other words everything works smoothly to achieve technical and allocative efficiency (see page 68).

● In reality no market works exactly like this. But by comparing them to the model of perfect competition, we can evaluate the way each market works.

The impact of market structure on pricing strategies

● Businesses in each of the market structures outlined above will require different approaches to pricing.

Competitive pricing

● Perfect competition will obviously require **competitive pricing**. With no product differentiation, keen prices are essential if the products are to sell at all. At a higher price, all possible customers would go to the seller offering the lowest price. At any price lower than that, the seller makes a loss.

Penetration pricing

● Businesses with **monopoly power** have choices. They can consider **premium pricing** or **price skimming**, if they want to get the highest possible price. However this may not be the profit maximising price. Total revenue may rise if they choose **penetration pricing**, tapping into a larger market. With economies of scale they may make more profit. If they want to drive competing producers out of business to strengthen their hold on the market, they may try **predatory pricing** although it is illegal.

> **Think!**
> What pricing strategies would appeal to a pharmaceutical company like GlaxoSmithKline which has patented drugs?

The impact of market structures on consumers

● Consumers are usually looking for the best bargain they can get. If prices are higher than they need to be, then they will be left with less spending power.

● Businesses are looking for the highest price they can get. They will charge what the market will bear. **Strong competition** keeps prices down so consumers can maximise the value they get from a given income.

Product differentiation

● Businesses like to avoid competition if they can and differentiate their products so that people may be attracted by the design, quality, taste or reliability of the product. This way they can charge a bit more. Many people will be happy with the value added by differentiation, especially if there is **monopolistic competition**, meaning that they get differentiated products but competition keeps prices fairly reasonable.

● Businesses in **oligopolistic markets** can use market power to control prices. Often but not always, they will be able to charge more than the product is really worth; this is why we have the CMA.

Non-price competition

Competition

The existence of non-price competition signals imperfect competition. It includes all kinds of product differentiation and also many aspects of marketing and promotion. Marketing strategies can create fashions in clothing, all kinds of household items and sometimes in the type of entertainment that people choose.

> **Example**
> Apple is differentiated from other electronic brands in obvious ways. The one thing it does not do is attempt to compete on price. It makes massive profits because it manages to provide new sources of customer satisfaction fast enough to attract regular repeat purchases.

The limitations of the model of perfect competition

Perfect competition describes a market in which producers react to customer demand. The market will be very responsive to changes in consumer preferences. Businesses that offer products for which demand is falling will in time leave the market and close down. (This is called allocative efficiency – see page 68.) It means that resources are used to produce exactly what is most in demand; nothing is wasted and consumers get what they want at a price that reflects the costs of production.

Imperfect competition

In the real world, most markets are imperfect and market failure is common. The way businesses respond to market forces depends on their market power. Market imperfections distort prices. Advertising distorts consumer preferences.

So perfect competition cannot tell us very much about individual businesses and markets. What it does – and this is important – is to give us a yardstick against which we can measure the impact of all the imperfections in real-world markets. It helps us to distinguish all the different ways in which actual market structures work.

4.1.2 Barriers to entry

Barriers to entry include all the difficulties that businesses are likely to face when they are setting up. We define a market where businesses can set up easily as **contestable**.

> **Contestable markets** are those that have low barriers to entry – new entrants can set up in business without having to invest serious amounts of capital. This can make a market competitive even though there are relatively few sellers.

Contestability and easy entry

Economies of scale

● In some markets, there are very few producers because economies of scale make large-scale production the most efficient. Smaller businesses trying to enter the market will fail because they have to charge more to break even. They simply can't compete with the big companies. To get big, they would have to start out with all the finance needed to benefit from economies of scale. Lack of finance is a barrier to entry.

● In other markets, very big companies can coexist with very small or medium sized ones. The small companies don't have economies of scale but this may not matter if their customer markets are quite small. The market is contestable even when it is dominated by a few big businesses because there is easy entry.

Examples
Some advertising businesses are very big indeed – like WWP and Saatchi and Saatchi. But advertising also has small businesses – tiny outfits with a rented office, a few computers and some imaginative people, some working freelance. Entry is easy.

Think!
Tech start-ups, e.g. producing new apps, often have very easy entry. Think of an example and explain how it happened.

New entrants

So long as it is possible for new entrants to come into the market in this way, it will be a contestable market. Existing producers will be deterred from charging very high prices and making big profits.

Sir Richard Branson, founder of the Virgin Group, started out selling vinyl records from the boot of his car.

Barriers to entry

> **Barriers to entry** are the factors that prevent firms from entering the market. Where there are many barriers to entry there will usually be less competition. **Easy entry** means being able to start up a new business without having to invest vast sums of money or comply with difficult regulations.

Barriers to entry include:

Differentiating

● **Product differentiation:** where competing products are both attractive and reasonably priced, a new product will either have to be carefully differentiated, or have a price advantage. This will require at least some financing.

● **Branding and brand loyalty** will have some influence on consumer preferences. Their choices may reflect long-standing habits which are hard to change. Large, well-established businesses will be well-known to, and trusted by, their customers.

● **Start-up costs** are often low for small businesses in the service sector and for craft production. But if expensive equipment is required the minimum efficient scale may be too high for businesses without financial backing. Also, sunk costs (such as advertising and equipment required) may land the start-up with big bills if it fails.

Patents

● **Intellectual property rights** are based on new ideas and inventions that can be protected by patents and copyright. These protect their originators from competitors – by law they cannot be copied without permission. They are legal barriers to entry.

● Products based on **R&D and technology change** will need funding before they can be brought to market. Even with good ideas, a small business will not be able to design and create a product without finance.

Example

In some markets entry is so easy that these problems do not arise. Richard Branson started out selling vinyl records from the boot of his car. He bought them cheaply because the major retailers had unwanted stocks and sold them at discounted prices. He was able to get started with almost no capital. Entry could not have been easier.

In many lines of business, start-up costs are high and entrepreneurs have to know how they are going to finance them. The higher the start-up costs the greater the risks. The bigger the project, the more need there will be for banks' involvement and a reputation in the field.

The impact of barriers to entry on market structure

● Markets will be contestable, and closest to perfect competition, where barriers to entry are the least significant. Businesses that specialise in selling to local markets and providing customer services on a relatively small scale may have no problem with barriers to entry because local advertising will attract interest without a big marketing budget.

Oligopolies

● Barriers to entry will be likely to lead to markets resembling oligopolies. They have the financial power for brand development and mass advertising.

● There are major barriers to entry for natural monopolies such as water supply because competition cannot actually reduce costs and prices.

● Global markets are often very competitive because businesses from many different countries can compete. They can break into new markets by selling existing products. If they are already well-established in their domestic markets, finance for expanded marketing can come from existing profits.

Economies of scale and their impact on cost and price

● Internal economies of scale cut production costs. Prices in mass markets for manufactured goods will tend to fall over time. This creates opportunities for many businesses to expand into new markets. These economies of scale include all forms of internal economies.

● Sometimes, external economies of scale can help new start-ups, usually where there are local facilities that benefit all producers. (For example, a pool of skilled labour or training schemes.) It is not uncommon for similar businesses to cluster in one area.

4.1.3 Oligopoly

Concentration ratios provide us with vital detail on oligopolies and the strength of their market power.

Concentration ratios

> The **concentration ratio** measures the extent to which a market or industry is dominated by a few leading firms. It is calculated by adding the market shares of the biggest firms in the industry. Adding together the three largest in the industry would be the three-firm concentration ratio.

Figure 1: Market shares, supermarkets, late 2015

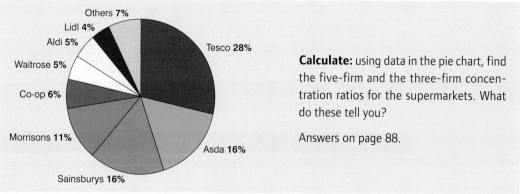

Calculate: using data in the pie chart, find the five-firm and the three-firm concentration ratios for the supermarkets. What do these tell you?

Answers on page 88.

Source: Wikipedia

Competition in an oligopoly; interdependence and price stability

Finding the supermarket concentration ratios shows clearly that this is an oligopoly. Yet we know that there are several in the 'other' category and numerous small delis and convenience stores that survive in spite of the oligopoly.

Inter-dependence

- The big supermarkets are interdependent in that they watch each others' prices all the time and there is significant competition. Some compete on price and some on quality and other aspects of non-price competition.

- Their advertising spend is quite high. Some compete by picking good locations. The big players have increased their market shares by setting up smaller stores that compete with convenience stores. So competition is somewhat limited.

- All are afraid of starting a price war. Probably, none would gain from this as profits would suffer. So there is a powerful tendency to compete on price but not too much, maybe just for a few lines, or for a short time. This means that there is a strong tendency to maintain fairly stable prices.

- Aldi and Lidl have recently been successful in increasing their market shares. This has made the market much less stable.

Most oligopolies share these features – think of the car industry, or other retail chains.

Tacit agreement

Tacit collusion

> **Tacit agreement** (or tacit collusion) refers to the understanding that develops between competing businesses. There is no personal contact and no formal agreement. The parties involved simply take no action that might increase the level of competition. They set their prices at roughly similar levels and stick to non-price competition.

Price makers

Price stability and tacit agreement go together. No one rocks the boat. This is very different from perfect competition where all businesses are price takers, charging the market rate. In an oligopoly, a seller with a significant market share can be a **price maker**. (This may be described as price leadership.) If one business raises its prices, the others will probably follow. All will choose from a range of pricing strategies. A damaging price war will often be followed by tacit agreement.

Price discrimination

Price elasticity of demand

- Within markets, there will be segments with differing price elasticities of demand. Big organisations can increase sales revenue by charging higher prices for a segment that has low price elasticity of demand and giving discounts for groups that are more price sensitive and have high price elasticity of demand.

- The obvious example is the railways with their railcards. Many others are able to distinguish between different groups of customers. The National Trust charges lower prices for older people and families and higher prices for individuals in work, who are likely to be less price-sensitive.

- The key factor is that it must be easy to identify particular groups of consumers. Also, to prevent people who can buy at a lower price from making a profit by selling on to those that are charged more.

4.1.4 Business objectives and pricing decisions

Average cost = Total costs ÷ Quantity sold

Average revenue = Total revenue ÷ Quantity sold

Profit = Total revenue – Total costs

Marginal cost and marginal revenue

Marginal cost (**MC**) is the cost of producing one more unit of output. **Marginal revenue** (**MR**) is the extra revenue that comes from selling one more unit of output.

Decisions at the margin

● Marginal costs and marginal revenue are important because businesses typically do not decide whether to carry on producing or close down. Usually they are thinking, shall we produce a bit more of this or a bit less? Comparing the extra revenue generated by producing a bit more, with the extra cost involved, makes sense.

● With perfect competition (or near it), the choice is simple. Producing more or less will not change the price. If we produce a bit more will it sell? The answer will be easy if occasionally they run out of stock and have nothing to sell for a while. Similarly, if the hairdresser often has to say that they are fully booked, they need to take on more staff. In both cases, marginal revenue could be higher than marginal cost, so profit will rise if they get the increase just right.

● Within an oligopoly the choice is more complicated. Producing more may mean that the market is flooded and prices fall. Before deciding, the business must estimate the likely fall in prices and decide what will happen to total revenue. With some market power, the business can have a degree of control over the market.

● Profit is maximised when MC = MR. If **MC < MR**, it will pay to produce more. If **MC > MR**, it will be best to produce less.

● Few business managers know about MC and MR, but they usually understand their markets instinctively and act in the way MC and MR suggest they should.

The link between marginal cost, marginal revenue and contribution

Contribution is the revenue from each extra unit sold minus its variable cost. It is the amount contributed to fixed costs by each additional sale. If fixed costs are already covered by earlier sales, it is pure profit. **Contribution is exactly like marginal revenue minus marginal cost.**

Another way of putting it:

Profit = (contribution per unit x quantity demanded) – fixed costs.

The impact of objectives on pricing strategies

Revenue maximising

● A sales or revenue maximising business will tend to think in terms of mass markets and penetration pricing or competitive pricing, or possibly cost-plus pricing. Small businesses will have less choice than those with some market power.

Profit maximising

● A profit maximising business will consider price skimming, or premium pricing. This is common with products that are relatively new or innovative, or where a business is targeting a new market. A business with first mover advantage has a lot of choice.

● A business with market power may use predatory pricing to drive competitors out of the market, even though this is illegal.

Think!
Individual business circumstances will vary greatly; you should be able to make more specific proposals in relation to a particular business. Think about Apple and then think about your local supermarket.

4.1.5 Productive and allocative efficiency

Efficiency

> **Productive efficiency** means minimising production costs by using the least possible quantity of real resources. This keeps prices to a minimum and helps to achieve the best possible standard of living. It fits neatly with the idea of lean production, minimising waste.
>
> **Allocative efficiency** is about using resources in such a way that actual output is perfectly matched to consumer preferences. It involves responding to changes in consumer demand as quickly as possible. It is achieved when resources are used to yield the maximum benefit to everyone. It is impossible to make anyone better off without making someone else worse off.

- In theory a free market system should satisfy both requirements. The forces of supply and demand encourage businesses to provide what people want, and to discontinue product lines that are no longer selling well. Resources are transferred, away from products that are no longer very popular, and used to produce the things people want most.

- This is allocative efficiency. No one much wants to buy coal to heat their homes as they did in the distant past; instead we get gas from the North Sea or import it in tankers from North America or the Middle East.

- Many businesses work hard to produce in more economical ways, so creating productive efficiency. Research and innovation cut costs, reduce the labour required, and often cut prices. (Think of washing machines and TVs.)

- This process often makes products more attractive as well as cutting costs. Losing a limb is not quite the disaster it once was because prosthetic limbs work so much better than a wooden leg.

Market imperfections

In practice, market imperfections do distort these processes. Market power can:

- shift from producing what we most want, to persuading us to buy something we did not know we wanted, or something different from what we prefer.

- push up prices by limiting output, keeping some products 'exclusive'.

- simply finding ways to avoid strong competition.

The significance of the margin; opportunity costs, tradeoffs and allocative efficiency

Allocative efficiency depends on businesses making changes at **the margin** all the time. If skirts are going out of fashion, production must be cut. New apps selling well will encourage people with the necessary technical skills to start up new businesses that can supply them. Similarly, if new production techniques are available it will pay businesses to adopt them in order to reduce production costs. The quest for profit leads to production being both economical and appropriate to needs and wants. Most of the decisions businesses take involve relatively small changes at the margin.

Consumer choice

Businesses will encounter **opportunity costs**. Change can be costly. They may feel they can carry on as they are, and the opportunity cost of change is a high risk strategy. Dynamic markets are like this. Risks do exist but with careful planning, businesses can explore the opportunity costs of the decisions that are open to them and survive.

Any time there is an opportunity cost there is a **trade-off**. We can choose either this, or that, but we cannot always have both. Dynamic markets are riskier than stable ones but they may also transform standards of living and reward entrepreneurs. What might the opportunity cost of the channel tunnel have been?

Where production decisions are not based on market forces, there is no profit signalling mechanism to flag up customer preferences. Choices about what to produce may be arbitrary. Resources are likely to be wasted on products for which there is little demand. Of course **allocative efficiency** does not guarantee a living wage for everyone. A functioning market system may well have many poorly paid people. It may also have significant numbers of very highly paid managers and wealthy shareholders. But dynamic markets do generally improve standards of living and inequality can be addressed through the tax system and government policies.

Increasing productivity to reduce average costs

Rising productivity is vital to a dynamic and growing economy. Higher productivity cuts unit labour costs and can increase pay. There are three basic routes to greater efficiency and increased productivity.

Process innovation

Technology: process innovation increases labour productivity, as do new technologies that lead to improvements in capital equipment. Shifting to a more capital intensive type of production raises labour productivity.

> **Example**
>
> A new generation of robots is coming into use in factories. They are called cobots, collaborative robots that work alongside people. They come from Rethink Robotics, a firm based in Boston, USA and made in Florida. They are lighter, more flexible and easier to program than their predecessors. Google Rethink Robotics now.

Multi-skilling

Human capital is the vital know-how that enables people to work efficiently. In general, the higher the level of skills, training and education, the more productive a human being will be. Partly this is due to greater flexibility – think of multiskilling. Some people can do a range of different jobs; they can be moved to wherever they are most needed.

Lean production

The **quality of management** is a key factor in productivity. The way people are organised can make a big difference to their output. Think of quality assurance, continuous improvement, cell production and other aspects of lean production. Sometimes the ethos of a business or good working conditions help to increase productivity. Businesses that pay their employees well and are trusted often say that it increases motivation and commitment and leads to higher productivity.

Figure 2: Labour productivity growth, 1973-2013

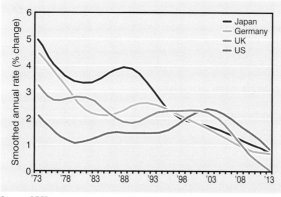

Source: OECD

Low productivity growth has in fact become a problem for many developed economies. Figure 2 shows how much productivity growth fell after 2000, despite the development of new technologies. After the financial crisis, many businesses cut back their investment programmes due to weak growth in demand for a wide range of products. This matters because as the boomer generation retires, labour may be in short supply and increased productivity will be needed to maintain current standards of living.

Matching the structure of production to the pattern of consumer preferences

● The great thing about the **market system** is that it rewards businesses for striving to produce the things that people want. These rewards – sales and profits – provide an **incentive** to create customer satisfaction. The system allocates resources in such a way that they are used efficiently. Under perfect competition there would be little evidence of greed in the business sector.

R&D

● In the absence of perfect competition we have **oligopolies** that can control the market and create wealth. However, these businesses spend vast sums on research, new product development and new ways of producing cheaply and efficiently. These developments benefit almost everyone, by bringing innovative products to market at prices that become more affordable as soon as **economies of scale** are achieved. (Most people in the UK have a mobile phone now.) Problems created by inequality can be dealt with through taxes and public spending, provided the voters agree.

Competitors must respond to ensure survival and continuing profitability. This is very obvious in the fashion industry.

Market orientation

● Many businesses do not produce exactly what people want – some produce what they hope you will want when you see it. This may work sometimes but it can lead to business failure. The way around this is to pay proper attention to **market research** and above all, to **market orientation**.

● Market orientation involves business in studying **consumer preferences** and keeping in close touch with their markets. There is also room for new ideas too, based on new technologies and imaginative design. This attitude has great potential for making a profit but it also benefits consumers. Careful **market segmentation** enables producers to cater for people on different income levels so that new technologies and designs benefit most people. **Innovative businesses** raise standards across the market because competitors have to strive for improvement in order to stay in business.

How markets interact with one another

Most businesses are both customers and suppliers.

Efficient suppliers

● **Supply chains** have become more and more complex in recent years. Outsourcing and offshoring have increased in importance. Businesses buy **intermediate goods** (components) that are needed in the production process. They also buy from specialists that can perform specific functions more cheaply than they themselves could. Each business depends heavily on its suppliers, to provide inputs of the correct standard, on time. If suppliers manage to cut their costs, they will help the customer business to compete more effectively. This happens all the time in the relationships between supermarkets and their suppliers.

● **Service sector** businesses are often part of a supply chain. They may also interact in other ways. Sometimes, if one cannot handle all of the business that is coming in, it will turn to a competitor to help. Consultancy businesses may buy in help with some work that requires expertise that they do not have. Architects work with construction companies.

● Most businesses are watching their **competitors** very closely. They will focus on both price and non-price competition. Any change in individual business strategies may affect the market. Consumers will be encouraged to switch to the superior or cheaper substitute. Competitors must respond in order to ensure survival and continuing profitability. This is very obvious in the fashion industry.

● For very big projects, a **consortium** may be put together. Construction companies will work together. Banks may club together to provide sufficient finance – as with the construction of the Channel Tunnel.

Chapter 8
Market power and market failure

> ⚠️ **WATCH OUT!**
>
> This chapter is about market failures that relate to different market structures, and how they might be mitigated by regulation. In Theme 1, you learnt about private, external and social costs and benefits and how government intervention can reduce their impact. Both chapters are about market failure but the contexts are different.

Terms to revise: business and stakeholder objectives (RG Theme 1, pages 3-5), the market economy, (RG Theme 1, pages 22-3 and 39-40), business growth (RG Theme 2, pages 57-62), marketing and elasticities (RG Theme 2, pages 68-72). Also keep in mind Chapter 7, Competition and market power in this book.

4.2.1 Market failure

Markets are usually seen as an efficient way of allocating resources, as long as competition is present to drive down costs and prices and provide consumers with choice and quality. In an efficient market the consumer has power and firms respond. But when market power begins to shift in favour of producers, they achieve a degree of **monopoly power**. This is one aspect of market failure.

Monopoly power

- Some prices will be higher than they need to be, reducing real incomes.

- Output may be restricted and the consumer loses out.

- Choice may be reduced and innovation slowed.

> **Market failure** occurs when there is an inefficient allocation of resources. Some potentially valuable resources are being wasted, i.e. not producing as much as they could do. Resources are being used inefficiently and consumers are less well off than they could be.

The significance of market power

Market power gives a firm some control over the market; it spends less time and effort competing. Competitive forces are reduced.

Market share

> **Market power** is the ability of a producer to exert some level of control over a market; this may include setting prices, restricting output, influencing other producers, creating barriers to entry and influencing suppliers. Where businesses can increase their market share they can usually also increase their market power.

Cartels

- Cartels are a form of anti-competitive activity. Their purpose is to increase prices and not actively compete with each other; as a result they directly affect the purchasers of their goods or services. They are illegal.

- Cartels have a damaging effect on the wider economy as they reduce the incentive for businesses to operate efficiently and to innovate.

> A **cartel** is any agreement within a group of businesses to reduce competition, avoiding competing with each other. The agreement is usually secret and may involve various strategies.

Cartels

Cartel members may agree on a range of issues:

- **Prices** may be fixed at a higher level than a competitive market would otherwise reach, or businesses may simply agree not to reduce prices and compete.

- **Output levels** can be fixed to restrict supply and thus force prices upwards.

- **Market sharing** could involve dividing up the market so that each member of the cartel has their own area, where the others do not intrude or compete.

- **Discounts and credit terms** can be fixed to disadvantage customers or suppliers.

- **Preferential supply** means restricting the number of customers and outlets they will supply. This makes the product more exclusive and forces up prices.

- **Bid rigging** means that cartel members may pretend to compete to win contracts but take it in turn to offer the lowest bid. This means they can charge much higher prices than if they were all competing genuinely to win the same contract.

Cartels are most likely to emerge in markets where competition is already limited, such as an oligopoly where several large firms dominate the market.

Collusion

Explicit or tacit

Collusion is closely linked to the operation of a cartel but it can take place between individuals or just two businesses. It does not have to entail a formal agreement.

- **Explicit collusion** involves two or more businesses discussing their plans and agreeing to follow a joint strategy. (It is different from a cartel, which is the term used when the participants can dominate the market and have a formal agreement.)

- **Tacit agreement** (sometimes called tacit collusion) is also possible. Competing firms may not communicate in any way. They simply keep their prices stable at roughly the same level. If both charge the same for equivalent products, prices will usually be higher than they would be if competition were strong. They avoid price cutting, but without actually meeting or having an agreement as such.

> **Explicit collusion** – occurs when there is a meeting or actual agreement to follow a joint strategy.

Restrictive practices

> **Restrictive practices** include any action that a business might use to limit competition. For example, they may try to enter into a market sharing agreement.

- Restrictive practices are used by cartels and colluding firms but they can also be used by individual firms, e.g. via preferential supply.

- Governments also have been accused of restrictive practices when industries are heavily regulated because this may restrict entry into the market.

- There are many different examples and more are being invented all the time.

Examples include…

- **Forcing retailers** not to stock a competitor's products.

- **Refusing to supply** retailers who discount products.

- **Tie-in sales**, where retailers are forced to stock a full range of the supplier's goods rather than just the best-selling ones. (This is also called full-line forcing.)

● **Exclusive dealing** occurs when a supplier requires or induces a customer to deal only, or mostly, in certain products.

● **Resale price maintenance** means suppliers force retailers not to discount prices.

Monopsony power

● Monopsony power exists when the buyer has power over the sellers; it is the opposite of monopoly power, where the seller has power over the buyers. Supermarkets have some monopsony power.

● The buyer is large enough to drive down the cost of inputs thus lowering the cost of production.

Single buyers

● Initially this may sound good because lower costs may mean lower prices but this does not consider the impact on suppliers who may struggle and pay very low wages to their workers.

● Monopsony power can translate into monopoly power if the advantages of monopsony give a business a competitive advantage and consumers may end up with less choice.

● For example many small booksellers have gone out of business because they cannot buy (and therefore sell) books as cheaply as Amazon can with its monopsony power.

Natural monopolies

● Natural monopolies exist when they are considered to be the most efficient form of market structure. Examples include the rail network and the national grid.

Duplication of resources

● Two sets of rail tracks or power lines would be wasteful. The capital costs of these systems and infra-structure are so high that a monopoly is the obvious answer.

● A natural monopoly is just as likely to use its monopoly power against the public interest as any other monopoly. The threat of competition makes people try harder to offer good value for money.

● Where there is no competition there is no pressure to be efficient. There is a danger of rising costs being passed on to the consumer.

● With no competition, investment in improvements may be too low and innovation may be slow or non-existent.

Power in the labour market

● There can be both monopoly and monopsony power in the labour market.

● A trade union or professional body can restrict the supply of labour to a particular industry or profession.

Monopsony employers may exploit their workers

● They can negotiate working conditions or force pay above free market wage levels, resulting in higher costs which will be passed on to the consumer in the form of higher prices.

● Monopsony employers can pay below free market wages because prospective workers have nowhere else to go to find employment.

● Examples include many public sector employees such as nurses and teachers.

The implications of market failure for consumers

Clearly, the anti-competitive and restrictive practices described above are very much against the interests of the consumer. They restrict competition and raise prices.

● If the consumer faces increased prices their disposable income is reduced. Their standard of living is effectively reduced.

● In addition customers may not have the same range of choice. Products may lack the innovation that a competitive market would achieve.

● *"Cartels take money off their customers by rigging markets against them,"* said Sir John Vickers, Director General, Office of Fair Trading, 2000-2005.

Future growth relies on new businesses being able to enter markets and grow.

The implications for businesses

Competitive-ness

Businesses may grow big and powerful and reap significant economies of scale that reduce prices to customers. However, they may also engage in restrictive practices that increase profitability. The more competitive a market is, the lower the profits. Businesses can go either way – use their power to invest in positive developments or use it to reduce competition.

In particular...

● If businesses do not face strong domestic competition, they do not become as efficient as they could be.

Profit vs. efficiency

● This weakens their competitiveness in international markets; exports may be disappointing and imports unnecessarily high.

● Restrictive practices are all about increasing profits and achieving a degree of monopoly power in the market.

● Competitive domestic markets often lead to a high level of innovation; this can be exceptionally profitable and lead to success in export markets.

The implications for governments

● The government has a responsibility to the **public interest** because that is whom they represent.

● The government also wants to achieve economic growth and that is slowed by market failure created by vested interests. This will impact upon international competitiveness.

● Future growth relies on new businesses being able to enter markets and grow. Businesses must be free to innovate; this can be stifled by market failure.

● The problem for governments is how to control or regulate market power and subsequent market failure.

● Government bodies can be faced with suppliers that have market power and overcharge them – e.g. when buying defence equipment.

● Bilateral monopolies, where powerful organisations employ people who all belong to a singe trade union, can present problems.

Example

The dispute between Southern Trains and the trade union RMT, causing intermittent strikes for many months in 2016, was definitely not in the interests of the customers.

Public interest

The **public interest** is a loose term but means the welfare or wellbeing of the public in general, as opposed to the selfish interests of individuals, groups and businesses. In the context of this course it means the interests of consumers and society in general, rather than the interests of businesses.

4.2.2 Business regulation

If markets were not regulated, it is highly likely that many businesses would act against the public interest. In the UK, anti-competitive behaviour is prohibited under a series of laws and regulations, implemented over several decades. The government intervenes in the market in a number of ways that protect the public interest. The main government agencies that implement competition policy are:

– The Competition and Markets Authority (CMA).

– The regulatory bodies.

– The EU Commission.

Ways of promoting competition

● Laws and regulations prohibit cartels and collusion, which entail **anti-competitive agreements** between businesses that want to reduce the forces of competition. They prevent the abuse by businesses of a dominant position in the market.

● Many different kinds of **restrictive practices** are prevented, e.g. market sharing and price fixing.

Controlling mergers and takeovers

● **Mergers and takeovers** that are likely to give the combined business 25% of the market are carefully investigated and may not be allowed to proceed with the merger, even if it is already agreed.

● Some such mergers are allowed to go through if the investigators think that they will not be a threat to customers. This is usually because the business has grown through its own efficient operations and its competitiveness so that the market remains both **contestable** and competitive.

● A 25% share of the market is classified as a legal monopoly because in most cases, it will give the business substantial **market power**. Some businesses have to sell off part of their organisation in order to keep within the limit.

● Some public companies have been **privatised** to ensure that markets are made more competitive. The most recent was Royal Mail, which now competes with a number of other parcel delivery businesses. This approach forces organisations with market power to become efficient by competing.

● Businesses that break competition law may face **investigation** and severe **penalties**.

Regulating natural monopolies

Many **natural monopolies** were in the past part of the public sector. This applied to water, electricity, gas, coal, the telephone system, the railways and others. They were privatised, mostly during the 1980s but retained some market power because duplicating pipelines, cabling and railway lines etc. is wasteful.

A **natural monopoly** occurs when the most efficient scale of production is a monopoly because more than one producer or supplier would involve wasteful duplication of resources.

Regulation

> A **regulatory body** is a public authority or government agency responsible for exercising auto-nomous control over a sphere of business activity. Regulators of natural monopolies were set up to ensure that natural monopolies do not exploit consumers by overcharging and do make strenuous efforts to keep their production costs down.

Examples

OFGEM oversees the energy companies. OFCOM is the communications regulator. ORR, the Office of Rail and Road, regulates the railway infrastructure and Highways England's management of the road network.

Regulators work closely with the organisations they are appointed to monitor. Their job is to ensure that a good service is provided at a reasonable price. However they share a great deal of information and they may be subject to **regulatory capture**.

> **Regulatory capture** occurs when the regulator is influenced by the industry's point of view. This happens easily because they are working closely together.

Protecting consumers

Consumers do not usually have any market power. They can boycott particular suppliers but this only works for them if they have good substitutes to choose from. Suppliers of consumer products have many ways of trying to fox their customers with misleading information.

- Inappropriate labelling can be very misleading.

- Pricing strategies can obscure the true cost of the product – especially if financing deals are on offer. (Think of the furniture outlets.)

Consumer protection law

- Price fixing by collusive businesses can leave consumers without the chance to buy from a competitor with a lower price. Tacit agreement may similarly deprive consumers of cheaper options.

- Before payday loans were regulated by the CMA, many people were tricked into borrowing more than they could afford to repay.

- Unfair contracts, e.g. when renting a home, may cause consumers to have to pay for hidden extras or accept poor quality accommodation.

- Consumers can be protected by regulation from poor quality products that may endanger them or be unreliable.

Regulators aim to ensure that companies do not exploit their monopoly power by charging excessive prices. They look at evidence of pricing behaviour and also the rates of return on capital employed to see if there is evidence of 'profiteering'. For example, recently the EU Competition Commission has enforced a number of cuts in the charges that can be made by mobile phone businesses when customers travel overseas.

The work of the Competition and Markets Authority (CMA)

On the 1 April 2014 the CMA took over many of the functions of the Competition Commission (CC) and the Office of Fair Trading (OFT) which had previously regulated businesses and markets. The CMA now has stronger powers than the Competition Commission had, to prevent mergers and also to reverse them after investigation.

> *"We work to promote competition for the benefit of consumers, both within and outside the UK. Our aim is to make markets work well for consumers, businesses and the economy."*
>
> (CMA website)

CMA

The CMA is responsible for:

● investigating mergers which could restrict competition.

● conducting market studies and investigations in markets where competition may be weak and consumer problems may develop.

● investigating where there may be breaches of UK or EU prohibitions in relation to anti-competitive agreements and abuses of dominant positions.

Penalising cartels

● bringing criminal proceedings against individuals who form business cartels.

● enforcing consumer protection legislation to tackle practices and market conditions that make it difficult for consumers to exercise choice.

● co-operating with sector regulators and encouraging them to use their powers.

● considering regulatory referrals and appeals from businesses that are suffering from the anti-competitive practices of their competitors.

Examples

In late 2014 the CMA announced an investigation into Pork Farms' acquisition of the chilled savoury pastries division of Kerry Foods, both of which supply supermarkets with own-label snacks. The CMA said the merger between the two firms had created the "realistic prospect" of "a substantial lessening of competition" in the supply of sausage rolls and cold and hot pies.

Investigations

"This merger will further reduce the choice available to retailers and consumers and may give the merged company the ability to raise prices or reduce the quality of these products."

In late 2016, the CMA found that five London modelling agencies – and the Association of Model Agents – had colluded on setting prices for modelling services. The CMA said "the parties exchanged information and discussed prices in the context of negotiations with particular customers." The offending businesses said the CMA was "wholly mistaken'. They were fined £1.5 million.

Penalties of up to 5% of turnover may be imposed on businesses that fail to comply with CMA requirements. In some cases, business managers can be sent to prison for their part in anti-competitive practices. Businesses that co-operate with the CMA can expect leniency even if they were involved in the offence.

As businesses become accustomed to CMA requirements in relation to anti-competitive practices, they will be rather less likely to offend.

Price fixing

Many price fixing cases are brought against groups of relatively small businesses. If they are producing intermediate goods of a specialised nature it is easier for them to get away with price fixing – at least until a competitor complains to the CMA.

In some cases, business managers can be sent to prison for their part in anti-competitive practices.

Impact of EU competition policy

The EU Competition Directorate, a part of the European Commission in Brussels (the EC), collaborates with national competition authorities (such as the CMA) to control cross-border practices that restrict competition. It enables all the competition authorities across the EU to pool their experience and work together. Frequently, the competition authorities in individual EU countries will collaborate with the European Commission and when necessary, also with the competition authorities in the USA.

The main difference between **competition law in the EU and in the UK** is that the EU focuses on issues that cross European borders and the UK focuses on issues that arise within the UK.

Example

The EC tackled Mastercard when it was found to be charging extra fees for cross-border card payments. These added to prices but gave no discernible benefit to the customer.

- The EC has a range of measures in place to protect the public interest. It is particularly useful in helping to control the activities of multinationals. Under EU rules, businesses:
  - May not fix prices or divide markets amongst themselves.
  - May not use a dominant position in a market to squeeze out smaller competitors.
  - Are not allowed to merge if that would put them in a position to control the market

Mergers within the EU

- Larger companies that do a lot of business in the EU cannot merge without prior approval from the EC – even if they are based outside the EU.

- The EU has wide ranging powers and can also impose large fines. (The EC has the power to impose fines up to 10% of global sales.)

- To date, the largest fine levied by the EC was £948m against Intel in 2009. The microchip maker was found to have offered financial incentives to manufacturers to favour its products over those of its rivals.

EU competition policy

- In the US, a business with a 60% market share will be investigated. In the EU, a market share of 38% is treated as implying unacceptable market power. These figures contrast with the UK, where 25% is described as a legal monopoly. However, in the UK evidence of a contestable market may mean that no action is taken even if the market share is above 25%.

Examples

One of the EU's best-known cases was against Microsoft. A 2003 EC ruling determined that Microsoft had unfairly favoured its own software over other competitors' by embedding it in the Windows operating system. Microsoft was fined £381m, followed by a further £194m in 2006 for failing to comply with elements of the original ruling. Rather ironically, in 2011 Microsoft went to the European Commission to lodge an anti-competition complaint against Google.

GlaxoSmithKline (GSK), the pharmaceutical giant, had a system of dual pricing. It charged one price in countries with higher incomes, and a lower price in countries with lower incomes. It was charging what the market would bear. The EU wanted a single price for all.

Employee protection

The government has over time introduced a series of laws to protect employees within the work environment. Failure by firms to comply with this legislation will result in prosecution. Compared to other European countries, the UK has a less regulated and more flexible labour force but regulation is needed to prevent serious injustice and poor working conditions.

Equality and fairness

- **Equal pay and equal opportunities** for men and women and for different ethnic groups create a fairer labour market in which employers must choose the best person for the job. There is ample research evidence that discrimination in favour of white males continues.

- **Minimum wages** – now the National Living Wage in the UK – reduce exploitation and poverty and create incentives to work.

- **The Working Time Directive** is an EU regulation that sets a maximum 48-hour working week.

- **The Health and Safety Act** has improved working conditions and provides for compensation where negligence has led to accidents.

- Strict rules help to prevent **unfair dismissal**.

Regulation can be expensive for employers but the lack of it can be costly for society. For example, poverty leads to poorer health and lack of health and safety regulation leads to accidents; both must be picked up by the NHS. Discrimination wastes talents and skills.

Example

Recent research shows that some employers still show a preference for hiring white males. This infringes applicants' rights; the employer is choosing not to select the best person for the job, as well as depriving many people of a fair wage. Employment protection law places great stress on equal opportunities. Over a period of several decades, laws and regulations have changed attitudes and non-compliance has been steadily reduced. This is a long-term project.

4.2.3 Arguments for and against regulation

The benefits of regulation

Increasing efficiency

- Without regulation, markets will be less efficient and show signs of market failure.
- Regulation helps to remove market imperfections and correct market failure.
- Competition creates a more robust and innovative economy, fostering economic growth by increasing efficiency.
- Regulation protects both consumers and employees.
- Businesses that are hurt by unfair competition can complain to the CMA, which will investigate.
- Regulation can benefit suppliers in a supply chain where monopsony buyers have market power and can force prices down.
- Better working conditions can help to raise productivity.

Level playing fields

- Having strict rules for all businesses levels the playing field. Socially responsible businesses may face competition from others that cut costs by paying very low wages and having very poor working conditions. Regulation for all means no business has a competitive advantage based on dubious labour market practices.

Productivity

As the market becomes more competitive businesses must strive against each other to make sales to consumers. This makes them efficient.

The community benefits from lower prices, greater choice, innovative products, improved reliability and better quality products and service.

The economy benefits as resources are used more efficiently as businesses strive to succeed. Productivity increases and businesses become more competitive internationally boosting exports and growth.

The costs of regulation

Compliance costs

- Imposing a regulatory framework will mean that government expenditure is necessary to create and run the regulatory bodies. This has an opportunity cost to the taxpayer.
- Implementing the legislation via the legal system can be costly for governments.
- Regulation by whatever means will impose compliance costs on businesses.
- For some businesses this may reduce profitability; they are forced to reduce prices or abandon mergers.
- This may reduce their ability to invest and grow in the future, to the detriment of the economy.
- Complying with consumer protection legislation such as health and safety may cause costs to be passed on to the consumer.
- Businesses tend to dislike regulation; it is likely to reduce profitability, especially if disregarding the regulations leads to fines or imprisonment.
- These costs must be weighed against the benefits of not allowing businesses to thrive by behaviour that puts others at a disadvantage.

Terms to revise: the profit signalling mechanism (RG Theme 1, pages 22-3), market failure, private, external and social costs and benefits, under-provision and under-consumption, government failure, (RG Theme 1, the whole of Chapter 1.5, pages 38-44).

Market failure in society

Chapter 8 deals with market failure in the context of the whole range of business structures. This chapter covers many other aspects of market failure.

Resource allocation

- When markets are working well, the **profit-signalling mechanism** leads to **allocative efficiency**.

- There is an optimum allocation of resources: all inputs are used in ways that generate the highest possible value. Output corresponds to consumers' preferences and their ability to pay for the goods and services they want.

- Market failure occurs when the allocation of resources does not fit the pattern of consumer demand. Businesses can use their market and monopoly power to alter the way market forces work. These kinds of market failure were covered in Chapter 8.

- The allocation of resources can be less than the optimum for many other reasons. The market may fail to produce enough of something that we do need (under-production, or under-provision). Also, markets may produce too much of something that we don't need (over-production).

- **Public goods** like the police force may not be provided because no one has an incentive to pay for it (under-production).

- **Merit goods** like education may not be available to all (under-production).

- **Demerit goods** may be available in much larger quantities than is socially desirable – e.g. tobacco products that create high social costs (over-production).

- **Externalities** – positive and negative – may create spillover effects (like pollution) that are not reflected in the price of the product.

Inequality

- Market forces may allocate resources in a way that leaves some people with a much lower **standard of living** than others'. Income inequality is found in markets that function freely.

- **Government intervention** can be used to try and correct market failure but this does not always work.

> **Example**
> Excess demand or excess supply conditions that persist for long periods indicate market failure. This can be because prices are sticky – they don't change in response to market pressures. But think about housing in the UK: planning restrictions (combined with nymbyism) restrict new building, prices rise and construction companies put off building in the expectation of even higher prices. Another example of persistent market failure is the long-lasting global excess demand for trained engineers.

The consequences of under-provision and under-consumption of merit and public goods

Market failure

> **Merit goods** can be provided by the private sector and often are, but the quantity that the free market provides is lower than the optimum level for society. They are under-provided by the market mechanism. Public sector action can remedy this.

- On an individual level, consumers make choices that do not necessarily lead to wider benefits for society.

- In the UK there are many private schools for those who are willing to pay the price. Similarly there are private hospitals and healthcare facilities available to those who can pay.

- *The problem is that many people would be unable to afford the prices of these services or would choose not to consume them and to spend their money on something else. This is not the best outcome for society as a whole.*

- Not educating some people would make our labour force much less competent than we require. Not dealing with health problems means more infectious diseases and much unnecessary suffering.

Public goods

> A **public good** is one that the free market will not provide at all. There is no incentive for a producer to supply it, it is impossible to charge for it and make a profit and it is impossible to prevent anyone else from consuming it for free.

Public goods are seen as beneficial and desirable features that a civilised society should have but they will not be provided by market forces. Common examples include national defence, street lighting, public parks and football pitches and clean air. Many public goods must be provided by the government because no other body has any incentive to provide them.

⚠ WATCH OUT!

Public goods are not called public because they are provided by the public sector (i.e. the government). Although rather confusingly they usually are!

Some jargon...
Public goods are said to be **non-rivalrous** and **non-excludable**.

Free-riders

Non rivalrous – when one person consumes a public good it does not affect or reduce the amount left for someone else to consume. For example, if I walk under a streetlight and benefit from the light it does not mean that the next person has less light.

Non excludable – it is impossible to prevent people who have not paid for a public good from consuming it. For example, I might pay for a streetlight outside my house but I cannot prevent you from walking by and using the light to see by without paying for it. This is the 'free-rider' problem.

Positive and negative externalities

- **Negative externalities** reflect market failure. Environmental problems are associated with external costs, as are congestion problems, which waste time and money.

External costs

- The cost of negative externalities is not covered by the price of the product. Third parties experience the external costs. They are spillover effects.

- For example, people with asthma suffer from the pollution created by vehicles. Fuel costs do not cover these external costs. Energy is over-consumed, compared to what it would be if the price were high enough to compensate the sufferers, reflecting the true social cost.

- **Positive externalities** provide benefits to people who did not buy the product. Some people spend money making their front gardens look good. The neighbours usually like this but don't have to pay for the plants.

- Externalities involve gainers and losers.

Over-consumption of demerit goods

As you might expect, demerit goods are the opposite of merit goods.

Negative externalities

> **Demerit goods** are overproduced by the free market, in quantities that are above the optimal level for society as a whole. They are the products that have bad effects on society. They are likely to produce expensive negative externalities such as health care needs, criminal activity and family breakdown.

Over-consumption

- Common examples include smoking, alcohol, recreational drugs, prostitution and gambling. All of these are considered to be socially undesirable in excess and likely to have a damaging effect on the productivity and wellbeing of society if left to the free market.

- Accordingly the government steps in to correct this market failure with a range of strategies including taxation, regulation and legislation. Sometimes the government creates an outright ban. These measures may reduce consumption levels.

Examples
The drug trade is subject to a legal ban. This probably reduces drug use, but it also has the effect of making drugs highly profitable because of the risks involved. Taxes on tobacco have been a factor in encouraging smokers to cut back or give up. Taxes on alcohol probably do reduce consumption to some extent. Gambling is carefully regulated.

Factor immobility (occupational and geographical)

The businesses and industries that we have today are very different from those of 50 years ago. Then secondary sector industries such as shipbuilding, engineering and steel-making were much more important, as were primary industries such as coal mining.

Structural changes

These industries have mostly gone and been replaced with service, financial and high-tech businesses. This is **structural change**. As much as changing demand, structural change is about where and how the output is produced.

The businesses and industries that we have today are very different from those of 50 years ago.

Structural change is not necessarily a problem if the labour market works. In theory, unemployed labour will move into those areas where there is high demand for labour and away from where it is no longer needed. The market would signal this by wage differentials. However labour is not always mobile and cannot easily move around the country or develop the skills necessary to cope with the changes. Labour markets can fail. Problems arise when there is:

Skills mismatch

- **geographical immobility of labour**, where labour cannot move to the areas where jobs are available, perhaps because of housing costs or family ties.

- **occupational immobility of labour**, meaning that unemployed people do not have the necessary skills and abilities to adapt to changing job requirements. This is called a skills mismatch.

Think!
Work out possible solutions to immobility and explain how they might, or might not work.

Imperfect and asymmetric information

Market failure occurs when one party has imperfect or asymmetric information. They are at a disadvantage when it comes to economic transactions and may make the wrong decisions due to lack of, or misleading information. This means that the market is not working properly and allocating resources as it should do, because one party can exploit their superior knowledge and the other may pay too much as a result.

How asymmetric information is used

> **Imperfect information** impairs the efficiency of markets because it leads to price distortions. Often buyers may pay more than they need to.
>
> **Asymmetric information** occurs when either buyers or sellers do not have full information. The party with the full information can benefit at the expense of the party without it.

Examples
The big six energy companies have recently been accused of making their bills and tariff charges too complicated, meaning that consumers cannot work out the best deal.

'Which?' magazine and its web site have reduced imperfect information.

'The market for lemons' explains everything. Google it and select Wikipedia. Seriously – you won't regret it.

Consequences of environmental change

Fossil fuel prices do not cover total costs

Environmental change is happening and it has economic consequences indicating market failure. It is estimated that it is costing the equivalent of 1.6% of global GDP. By 2030 that is forecast to rise to 3.2% of global GDP, with the world's least developed countries suffering losses of up to 11% of their GDP. Rising sea levels mean that low-lying islands are already preparing to lose everything. In time, most of the big cities located close to the sea are likely to face very serious difficulties.

> Sheikh Hasina, prime minister of Bangladesh, where huge areas of very low-lying land had been flooded, said: *"For us, it means losing about 4m tonnes of food grain, amounting to about $2.5bn. That is about 2% of our GDP. Adding up the damages to property and other losses, we are faced with a total loss of about 3-4% of GDP. Without these losses, we could have easily secured much higher growth."*

Vested interests

It seems likely that fossil fuel use is not going to decline quickly. Likely negative externalities include the effects of pollution and congestion, the way warmer temperatures will affect agricultural production and the need to provide help for people in coastal regions. Appropriate taxes on energy products could help but vested interests may prevent remedial action aimed at reducing negative externalities.

4.3.2 Externalities

● Some transactions involve **external costs** and **external benefits** for third parties, people who neither bought nor sold the products in question.

● External benefits are paid for but third parties usually get the benefits for nothing.

● In free markets, the price normally reflects just the **private costs and benefits** of goods and services.

● Negative externalities (external costs) are not reflected in private costs.

● **Social costs** include both external costs and private costs. If there is a negative externality social costs will be higher than private costs, reflecting the true cost of production.

● The market may 'fail' to take into account all the external costs involved. The consumer is not paying the full (social) cost of production.

● **Social benefits** may be provided by governments.

Externalities can be negative or positive. If you benefit from a good education and become a doctor or teacher you will benefit on a personal level but society will also benefit from your actions.

The impact on society of charging prices that do not reflect social costs

Market prices = private costs

● Market prices are generally based on the internal (private) costs involved and ignore external costs. This means that the prices of products with negative externalities will be lower than they should be, causing more to be consumed (over-consumption). This distorts allocative efficiency and can have a negative impact on society.

● The people who benefit are the producers and consumers of the product concerned. Over-consumption based on private costs will yield more profit than it would if price was based on social costs. Market-based prices mean consumers get more for their money.

● The losers are the people who suffer from the external costs. These will often be directly related to pollution or toxic waste, but they may also affect people who suffer from the excess demand for public services that are overwhelmed by those suffering from negative externalities.

Environmental externalities

It is notoriously difficult to place a value on environmental problems but it is clear that environmental externalities are a major cause of market failure. The price of tropical hardwoods has in the past only reflected the private costs of cutting and distributing the timber. No account was taken of the external costs of losing large areas of precious rainforest. This meant that more wood was consumed than should have been, given the negative impact on society of the loss of rainforest. There are many examples like this

It is notoriously difficult to place a value on environmental problems but it is clear that environmental externalities are a major cause of market failure.

where there will be over-consumption and extra negative externalities such as pollution because the polluter does not have to pay for the full costs to society.

Taxing polluters

If the price were to reflect external costs as well, it might go some way towards correcting market failure. This is the **Polluter Pays Principle**. A tax can be placed on the product that creates the negative externality; the tax revenue can pay for measures to reduce the scale of the problem. This is described as internalising an external cost. (See also tradable pollution permits, page 87.)

Example
Taxes on petrol, together with the price paid, could cover the full social cost it creates. Tax revenue could be used to fund research into reducing carbon emissions.

It can be hard to link externalities to the consequences that people experience. Where water is contaminated, the impact on people whose occupation is in the fishing industry will be significant. But how do you identify the causes of the contaminated water? It could come from agriculture or industry or just from people needing to dispose of waste water.

4.3.3 Policies to deal with market failure

Measuring external costs

Some externalities are relatively easy to measure. If we look at car use, we can probably estimate the costs of accidents, wear and tear on the roads and lost productivity to businesses as employees sit in traffic jams and so on. We can then add these external costs to the private costs of motoring by increasing the car tax and so 'correct' the market failure. This is already starting to happen.

Example
Quantifying the cost of slow travel and gridlocked roads led to the London congestion charge. Users have to pay to drive into the congestion charge zone during the working day.

● Where external costs cannot be quantified, solutions may be harder to find. Even if we can reach a figure for external costs, it will be open to dispute. How could we measure long-term damage to the climate, caused by vehicles?

● There is a real problem here. Where there are negative externalities that are clearly significant but cannot be quantified, it is difficult to decide how much to spend on solutions. Political issues arise.

The provision of public and merit goods

When there are clear signs of under-production and under-consumption, we need to consider the role of public and merit goods.

● Society gets the benefits of public goods – they are available to all. The government uses tax revenue to cover the cost because they must be provided collectively or not at all.

Under-production

● Public goods meet basic needs that keep us safe; they include the legal system, defence, roads, the fire service and so on. These are externalities in the sense that everyone benefits, regardless of how much tax they pay.

● Merit goods also provide external benefits – a better educated population helps to make the economy more competitive, which benefits all, including employees and exporters.

● Direct provision by the government is the simplest way to provide merit goods. This is what happens in the UK with state education and the National Health Service.

But... voters have a habit of disliking taxes. In 2016, in Germany, the USA and the UK there were bridges and roads badly in need of repair or replacement. Governments resist raising taxes even when the need for public and merit goods is clear.

Indirect taxation of demerit goods

● One way to provide an incentive to change behaviour is to alter the price.

Indirect taxes

● Indirect taxation refers to taxes that are added to selling prices. VAT is an indirect tax, as are the excise taxes that are applied to specific products.

● The imposition of a tax on certain goods and services will increase the price and reduce consumption.

● Demerit goods such as alcohol and tobacco carry excise taxes that discourage consumption and in turn reduce some of the negative externalities they produce.

● The imposition of a tax shifts the supply curve vertically upwards by the amount of the tax (it appears to shift to the left, see Figure 1).

● Price has increased from P1 to P2 and quantity demanded falls.

● The amount of the fall depends on the price elasticity of demand for the product.

Figure 1: Price inelastic demand and tax

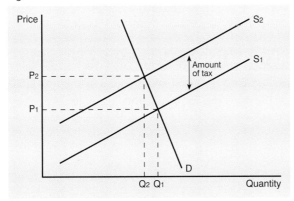

Example

Figure 1 fits the past situation with tobacco quite well. With no substitute for tobacco, addiction meant that demand was inelastic. Higher taxes did reduce tobacco use but not by much. In fact, tobacco taxes provided substantial tax revenues.

Taxing where there are substitutes

Then a substitute was invented – vaping. You would expect a change in the price elasticity of demand for cigarettes. The outcome might look like Figure 2.

Figure 2: Price elastic demand and tax

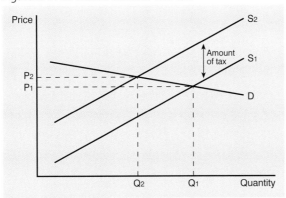

Tradable pollution permits

Tradable permits are usually used as a way of reducing carbon emissions. The government issues a restricted number of permits equal to the desired level of emissions.

Encouraging efficiency

- Each emitter is given a licence to release a specified number of tons of the pollutant.

- Businesses that own the permits may then either retain them and release the pollutants, or reduce emissions and sell the unused permits.

- The fact that the permits have value as an item to be sold gives the owner an incentive to become more efficient and reduce their emissions.

- Efficient producers should be able to expand without needing to buy more permits.

- Inefficient producers will have to buy more permits if they want to expand. This increases their operating costs and makes it harder to compete.

- The system should encourage efficiency and a reduction in negative externalities.

- Alternatives to tradable permits include carbon taxes and planting more trees.

- The system will work provided the number of permits is restricted to ensure that businesses do actually have to reduce emissions.

Provision of information

Reducing asymmetric information

- Changes in consumer behaviour can be brought about by either direct education in schools or by campaigns to raise awareness of issues. For example people are much more aware of the need to conserve energy and the environment than they were 20 to 30 years ago.

- Modern technology can reduce asymmetric information on behalf of the consumer. At the swipe of a finger consumers can now check prices and read reviews before making decisions.

- Price comparison websites help, as do sites such as Money Saving Expert that give full information for the consumer.

- Social media links consumers and enables information to be shared.

- Pressure groups such as The Consumer Association (Which?) act to correct market failure by providing information to consumers.

Legislation and regulation

Legal restrictions

- Governments can control negative externalities to some degree with laws or regulations. They can pass laws that change behaviour. They can be used in a wide variety of contexts, to control both individual and business activity e.g. setting acceptable pollution levels, or making the drug trade illegal.

> **Legislation** simply refers to laws passed by Parliament. By-laws can be passed by local councils.
>
> **Regulation** can be used as a general term to refer to laws and regulations, but usually, it means rules concerning what businesses and other organisations can and cannot do. Most regulations are imposed by governments. However, some industries and professions have their own rules. This is known as self-regulation.

- Regulation includes all the rules that apply to businesses and also to some public sector activities. These may relate to the environment, health and safety, consumer and employment protection or competition.

- For the law to be effective, sanctions must be sufficient to deter unlawful behaviour. Failure to comply will result in the imposition of a penalty.

Enforcing regulations

Examples

The UK Environment Agency sets out all the regulations that affect the environment in the UK. It handles the enforcement of a huge range of regulations all the way from fishing rod licences to the rules for the disposal of hazardous waste. If a business buys, sells or transports waste products it must register with the agency. OFGEM is another example.

The Water Act of 2003 built on previous pieces of legislation and established a new regulatory board along with a new independent Consumer Council for Water.

The impact of these policies on the economy and society, long- and short-term

The government intervenes to protect the public interest, but just how effective are its policies? It decides on the extent to which negative externalities will be permitted and the appropriate sanctions, should the law be broken or regulations infringed.

Have public interest issues been enhanced?

Market failure and regulation

- The first environmental control, the Clean Air Act of 1956, was carefully monitored and widely accepted.

- However, some laws are ignored. An irresponsible business may consider it cheaper to pollute and pay a fine every now and then rather than go to all the expense of cleaning up its production process. The sanctions may simply be a price worth paying.

- De-merit goods such as illegal drugs are still available; underage drinkers still consume alcohol and so on.

- Environmental protection has had an effect, though probably not enough yet to avoid big future problems.

- Nevertheless legislation clearly has an important role to play in correcting some market failures. Laws and regulations can change attitudes.

Answers to question on page 65:

The five-firm concentration ratio is 77%.
The three-firm concentration ratio is 60%.

Terms to revise: the economic cycle, circular flow of income, inflation and unemployment, all in RG Theme 2, pages 94-103. Monetary, fiscal and supply side policies, all in RG Theme 2, pages 104-111.

4.4.1 The AD/AS model

You met the aggregate demand/aggregate supply diagram in Theme 2, section 2.5, along with the economic cycle and the circular flow of money. On the face of it, they look like three different things. In fact they do all fit together:

● The economic cycle tells you about the way the economy fluctuates over time.

● The circular flow of money identifies the component parts of aggregate demand.

● The AD/AS diagram can be used to represent the situation in the economy at a particular time – a snapshot that helps you to identify some causes and effects (and show the examiner that you understand all these things).

● Start with $AD = C + I + G + (X - M)$.   If you don't feel very familiar with all this, work on Terms to revise (above) and study the Theme 2 content, NOW.

Changes in Aggregate Demand (AD) and Aggregate Supply (AS)

At the end of 2016, the UK economy looked like this:

Using diagrams to explain change

Figure 1: AS and AD with low inflation and low unemployment

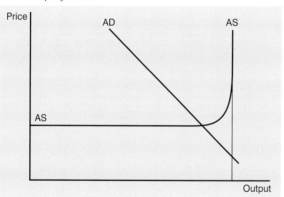

Notice that this is not like the standard version of an AS/AD diagram. The economy is close to full employment. Unemployment is 4.8%. Most of this can be explained by frictional unemployment – the natural turnover of people changing jobs and retiring. The workforce was at an all time high of 32 million.

Looks good doesn't it. However two things were expected. One was that investment might fall because of nervousness about Brexit (and it wasn't high in the first place). Not many business people felt like taking big risks. FDI was probably falling. An increase in AS needs strong investment.

The other major factor was the dramatic fall in the exchange rate after the EU referendum. You know what happens after depreciation. Exports rise but only after a time lag (spread over two years). Import prices rise, after a much shorter time lag – perhaps six months, the time for which importing businesses have bought currency forward, to reduce risks.

Try this

Work out what this might mean. What will happen to aggregate demand? Draw an AS/AD diagram to show what you think. If you can think of more than one possible outcome, draw two diagrams. Talk over your conclusions with a friend who is revising the same thing. If you are reading this after the end of 2017, try doing the same thing for the present day.

Summarising:

Connecting causes and consequences

● Any change in the components of aggregate demand will change the total. Rising consumption, government spending, investment and exports all shift AD rightwards. Rising savings, taxes and imports will shift AD to the left and growth will slow.

● Aggregate supply will increase (shift to the right) if the workforce is growing (inward migration, especially if the migrants have skills), if education and training facilities improve, or if investment is growing and new technologies are creating extra capacity.

● AS and AD interact. A change in either one of them will alter the level of output.

● The whole AS curve will shift upwards if inflation is raising prices.

If both AD and AS are growing, unemployment and inflation might stay about the same. But if import prices rise, and business costs rise wherever inputs are imported, the whole AS curve will shift upwards because whatever else happens, prices will rise at every level of AD. See Figure 2: AD will fall, because the rise in prices causes a movement along the AD curve (see the arrow).

Figure 2: Price rises shift AS upwards, but capacity is not growing

AS and inflation

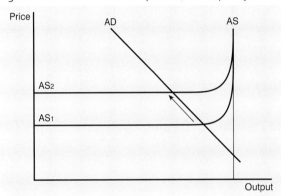

Exam tip

For simplicity, we assume in Figure 2 that AD stays the same. It is not a good idea to try to illustrate two changes on the same diagram. If two things are changing, draw two separate diagrams, one for each change.

Full capacity output

In Figures 1 and 2 you can see full capacity output. It's the vertical part of the AS curve. It's the most that can possibly be produced, given the available resources. Besides investment, training, new technologies and migration, there are a few other things that can raise potential full capacity output. Freeing up land for development (changing the planning laws), better infrastructure and the discovery of new resources (e.g. oil, gas, or any mineral deposits) which all contribute to capacity output and economic growth.

Productive capacity

● **Full capacity output** is the maximum output that can be produced when all available resources are fully employed. This can happen when AD is rising, unemployment is low and the economy is growing.

● **Actual output** will be determined by AD. In a recession there will be underutilised resources because AD has shifted to the left and firms have cut production.

Impact of changes in AD and AS on inflation and unemployment

Rising AD will lead to economic growth, for as long as there is spare capacity in the economy. The dynamism of the economy will encourage more injections into the circular flow.

● As AD gets close to full capacity output, shortages (sometimes called bottlenecks) will develop. Skilled people will be scarce, maybe also other inputs. The number of job vacancies will increase. Wages will rise as employers compete to recruit the people they need. Inflation will accelerate.

Vacancies

Figure 3: Vacancy rates, UK, 2001-2016

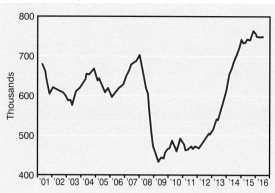

Source: ONS

Vacancy rates give a very clear indication of tightness in the labour market, of the economy's closeness to full capacity output, and of the extent of skill shortages.

● Once output grows beyond the point where the AS curve turns upwards (see Figure 1), inflation rises, accelerating further as skill shortages develop.

Rising AD

● Imports may rise as incomes are relatively high; exports may fall when businesses find they can sell more of their output in the domestic market.

● The strength of demand means that businesses can raise their prices and still sell the product. Profits will rise.

● Unemployment will be very low.

● Once AD reaches the full capacity output line, output cannot increase any further in the short run.

Turning point

At this point, the economy will probably change direction – it is at a turning point in the economic cycle. There will be concern about rising inflation rates. The government will probably implement contractionary policies. (See pages 95-6.)

● Higher taxes will reduce spending on both domestic products and imports.

● High interest rates will discourage investment.

Slowing AD

● Nervous people may try to save more. Falling injections and rising leakages from the circular flow of money will reduce AD. This will reduce the 'overheating' in the economy.

● Falling demand will lead to redundancies. Vacancies will rise. New start-ups will diminish. Unemployment will rise.

● After a while, inflation will ease up. Real incomes will be falling, consumers will spend less and businesses will cut prices in order to compete.

● Unemployment will become a big problem causing widespread distress. Government policies will become more expansionary.

If inflation is controlled, this boom and bust sequence may not happen. Steady growth may be possible. But this requires that GDP grows steadily, not fast. This happened in the Great Moderation, between 1996 and 2007, but it did not survive the financial crisis in 2008-9.

The multiplier effect

When an economy is growing, rising injections have a knock-on effect, leading to a further increase in aggregate demand. It works like this:

A rise in investment leads to orders for new machinery → Manufacturers take on more labour → New employees take home more pay → They spend it on (say) takeaway meals → The takeaway needs more employees

Multiplier

This continues as increased spending generates more income and more spending. This is the multiplier effect. Eventually the increased spending leaks away as people pay more tax, buy more imports and maybe save more. A downward multiplier will operate in a recession.

The multiplier is important. Governments that are planning expansionary policies must be careful not to inject too much stimulus into the economy. Getting the desired effect will take time.

How the AS/AD model sheds light on the economy as a whole

The AS/AD model can help to explain the factors that influence economic growth, incomes, inflation and unemployment. But we have to be aware of all the other major influences on the domestic and the global economy. The AS/AD model can be used to predict short run or long run changes – which may differ.

The model can…	When other factors and influences are at work, we have to use the model very carefully…
Show the effect of a change in an injection or a leakage.	To get the full picture we must also consider:
Predict the impact of change on output, employment and prices.	• the impact of globalisation and changes in trading relationships.
Explain the effect of changes in technology, or even natural disasters.	• business reactions to uncertainty.
	• changing levels of inequality.
Illustrate aspects of the economic cycle.	• abrupt changes, e.g. falling or rising oil prices.
	• changes in fiscal and monetary policies.

4.4.2 Demand-side policies

Demand-side policies directly affect the level of aggregate demand. The basic expectation is:

Stimulus

● If the economy is sluggish or in recession, increased AD will stimulate business activity and foster economic growth.

Contraction

● If the economy is overheating, skill shortages are a problem and inflation is on the rise, then AD can be reduced so that the economy can grow more slowly.

The distinction between monetary and fiscal policy

Fiscal...

Fiscal policy is determined by the government of the day.

● It can be used to address short-term problems.

● It may require changes to taxation or government expenditure. Changes in direct taxes (mainly income and corporation tax), VAT and other indirect taxes, can influence AD.

● The government can stimulate the economy with tax cuts and/or increased government expenditure, or reduce inflation risks by raising taxes and cutting public expenditure.

● Fiscal policies can also be used to help fund new research and technologies, to build infrastructure and to address problems relating to inequality, health care and education.

...and monetary policy

The Bank of England is independent of the government. **Monetary policy** is determined by the Monetary Policy Committee, which is part of the Bank of England. (See page 105.)

● This removes political influence from these very technical decisions. The government cannot reduce interest rates in the run-up to an election.

● The MPC uses **interest rates** to keep inflation close to the target rate. The government decides the target percentage; the Bank of England sets **base rate** accordingly but keeps in close touch with the government. When base rate changes, the effect ripples across all interest rates.

Unconventional monetary policy

● **Asset purchases** began after the financial crisis of 2008-9. They are often referred to as **quantitative easing** (**QE**). They increase the money supply by making it easier for banks to lend to businesses to fund investment. They work when interest rates are so low that they cannot be reduced further. This is another way to stimulate the economy. It is controversial, partly because it will not increase investment if uncertainty causes businesses to cut back on investment.

> The **base rate** is the interest rate at which the Bank of England lends to the banks, whenever they are short of cash and need overnight or very short-term loans.
>
> **Quantitative easing** (asset purchases) is an alternative monetary policy that allows the Bank of England to buy bonds from the banks, so that they can provide more finance for investment. It is designed solely to stimulate the economy when interest rates are generally very low.

The impact of changing the level of AD on the economy as a whole

Expansionary policy

Expansionary policies include both fiscal and monetary policies that can increase AD.

● Individuals get more disposable income, through lower taxes, lower mortgage payments and maybe higher welfare benefits. Some disposable income may be saved but much will be spent. This gives businesses an incentive to expand production.

● Increased government expenditure will fund public investment and public services. Low interest rates will encourage private investment, creating more jobs and raising incomes.

● The multiplier effect will encourage faster economic growth. Imports may increase due to higher incomes. In time, inflation may accelerate.

Contractionary policy

If the economy has been growing unsustainably fast, **contractionary policies** may be introduced. Tight fiscal and monetary policies will cause AD to fall; the economy will grow more slowly.

● Some employees will be made redundant. Their incomes and consumer spending will fall.

● New investment may look risky. Businesses will become more cautious as profits fall.

● Exporters may try harder to sell abroad because of the weak home market.

● Government expenditure cuts will also reduce employment and spending. There will be a downward multiplier effect.

Quantitative easing is designed solely to stimulate the economy when interest rates are generally very low.

The use of AD/AS diagrams to illustrate demand-side policies

Figure 4: Aggregate demand at three different stages

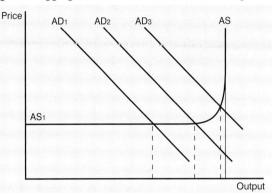

Growth – but not too much

- In Figure 4, AD1 shows a situation in which there is a serious recession. Output is very low and the economy needs to be stimulated with expansionary policies.

- AD2 shows the effect of an expansionary policy. Output is much higher and unemployment will be lower. Everyone will feel better off. Inflation is still low.

- At AD3, the expansion has continued but now output is close to full capacity. Inflation will be accelerating, partly because of skill shortages and pay demands but also because businesses can raise prices. Demand-side policies can help to slow the rate of economic growth.

- Rather than encouraging boom and bust, policy should be kept steady to encourage moderate growth and a stable economy.

How investment, job creation and economic growth can be encouraged

Sustainable growth

- One way to maintain stable, sustainable growth is to create a policy package. This will include some fiscal and monetary policies, carefully considered and implemented so that they do not lead to over-full employment and inflation.

- To this can be added supply side policies that will increase aggregate supply (see pages 96-98). They might include better training, infrastructure development, encouragement of R&D and innovation and incentives to invest and to work. These and other approaches help to increase the productive capacity of the economy. This is usually better than relying entirely on aggregate demand to stimulate production.

How inflation and unemployment can be controlled

Inflation can be controlled by reducing aggregate demand. If it is accelerating fast, then fiscal policy *must* be used because swift action is required. However, it is much better to act earlier, when economic growth is easier to slow. This is why the MPC reviews the base rate every month. The aim is to keep the inflation rate close to 2%.

Inflation can be kept steady in the long-term by using supply-side policies to increase capacity. When aggregate supply is rising steadily, inflationary pressures are reduced, especially if there is strong competition across much of the economy. Competition policy helps and competing imports reduce the extent to which businesses can raise prices.

Unemployment can be cut by increasing aggregate demand. This works really well if the unemployment is cyclical, i.e. related to the economic cycle. (Cyclical unemployment is the same as demand deficiency unemployment.) If structural unemployment is the main problem, increasing AD will not work. The unemployed need retraining and homes where there are vacancies, as well as incentives to work.

Time lags involved

Almost all economic policies involve time lags, which must be allowed for by policy makers.

● People – individuals and businesses – take time to adjust. If the policy is to create an incentive to invest, businesses will take years to plan and implement investment projects.

Unemployment is lagged to the economic cycle

● Unemployment increases 1-2 years after a fall in AD and similarly recovers slowly after a recession. In a recession, businesses hang on to their best employees if they can, in the hope that sales will soon pick up again. When sales improve, they wait to be sure that the change will last before recruiting more people.

● Tax cuts are different – they are likely to raise spending almost immediately.

Strengths and weaknesses of demand-side policies

Strengths of demand-side policies

● Tax cuts can be implemented quickly.

● Can stimulate the economy if AD < AS.

● Contractionary policies can prevent overheating if AD > AS.

● Progressive taxes together with welfare benefits adjust when AD changes and act as **automatic stabilisers**. If income is falling, tax revenue falls and unemployment benefits rise, and vice versa.

Weakness of demand-side policies

● It is difficult to stimulate the economy or slow it down with exactly the right amount of policy change which can be destabilising.

● Time lags make it hard to predict the eventual outcome.

● It may be unwise to cut taxes or increase public spending if the government already has a big public sector deficit.

● If unemployment is structural, demand-side policies will not help.

Potential policy conflicts and trade-offs facing policymakers when applying policies

● The problem for the government is that the four main economic objectives – sustainable economic growth, low unemployment, low inflation and low balance of payments deficits – are often incompatible with each other. There are policy conflicts.

Demand-side policies can overshoot

● Attempts to resolve one problem create problems elsewhere – it is difficult to keep both unemployment and inflation low at the same time.

● Expansionary policies reduce unemployment but as output approaches full capacity, inflation will accelerate. Contractionary policies will dampen AD and reduce inflationary pressures but will also increase unemployment.

● Economic policy often involves **trade-offs**.

Attempts to resolve one problem create problems elsewhere – it is difficult to keep both unemployment and inflation low at the same time.

> **Trade-offs** occur when two objectives cannot both be achieved at once. The more you have of one variable the less you have of another.

Policy objective	Intended result	Possible dangers
To increase the economic growth rate with expansionary policies.	AD increases, unemployment falls, the multiplier effect leads to higher output and more jobs.	Growth may cause inflation to accelerate. As AD and incomes increase, imports may increase and lead to a balance of trade deficit.
To reduce inflation with contractionary policies.	Inflation slows, exports may increase as they become more competitive; the balance of trade improves.	Contractionary policies slow down economic growth so that unemployment increases.
To reduce unemployment with expansionary policies.	Increased AD reduces unemployment. With more people working, AD may increase further.	Growth may cause inflation to accelerate. As AD and incomes increase, imports may rise and worsen the balance of trade.

Time lags complicate policy outcomes

These trade-offs are inevitable when governments use expansionary and contractionary policies to influence the level of aggregate demand. However, supply-side policies can provide benefits that help to reduce the policy conflict, provided allowance is made for time lags.

4.4.3 Supply-side policies

The distinction between market-based and interventionist methods

Crucial factor: all supply side measures take time to have an effect. (Think of improving primary school teaching – very likely indeed to improve employability, 20 years later.) So if the economy needs action now, or over the next two years, demand-side policies will be more useful.

- Supply-side policies are designed to increase productive capacity and use resources more efficiently. They aim to raise productivity levels. They help to keep AS growing.

Free market policies

- Some supply side policies are suited to a **market-based economy**, in which government is kept 'small', with minimal interference in economic and business decision-taking.

- In contrast, **interventionist policies** involve government decisions and policies that seek to have a direct influence on the wellbeing of both people and businesses.

- Economists and politicians differ – some favour interfering as little as possible (the free-market approach). Others favour an interventionist approach (so the government intervenes to achieve both good employment levels and low inflation).

Market based and interventionist policies

The table below indicates market based and interventionist policies with similar objectives. All the above supply-side policies can be useful in fostering greater efficiency in the use of resources. However market-based policies may lead to greater inequality and possible tensions in society, neither of which is helpful in creating flexible and efficient markets.

Efficient use of resources

Other supply-side possibilities include:

- Developing a flexible labour force; reducing structural unemployment by dealing with immobilities.

- Encouraging research and development (R&D), funding projects of particular importance. (Investing in medical developments with potential to reduce NHS costs can do much to make health care more efficient.) New technologies can increase AS considerably.

- Supporting R&D generally can encourage investment, enhancing productive capacity.

- Deregulation – to reduce the extent to which businesses are hampered by restrictions.

Alternative approaches

Supply side objectives	Market based policies	Interventionist policies
Increasing incentives	Cutting taxes and reducing welfare benefits to create an incentive to work.	Using tax credits to ensure that everyone is better off in work.
Promoting competition	Reducing trade barriers, de-regulation.	Implementing competition policy to reduce restrictive practices and market power.
Reforming the labour market	Reducing employment protection and trade union power; privatisation.	Regulating business practices. Helping unemployed people to find appropriate jobs.
Improving employees' skills	Training within the business.	Training in colleges.
Improving infrastructure	Using private sector funds.	Increasing public expenditure.

The use of AD/AS diagrams to illustrate supply-side policies

Successful supply-side policies shift the AS curve to the right. They allow AD to grow faster without setting off inflation. Notice how AS1 and AD1 in the diagram allow growth in output up to B, without inflation becoming a problem. If productive capacity increases to AS2, output can expand to C, achieving both growth and stability.

Growth and stability

Figure 5: Impact of successful supply-side policies

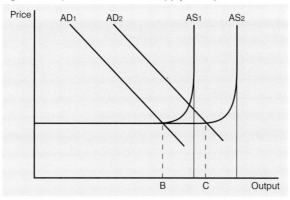

Strengths and weaknesses of supply-side policies

Policies for the long term

● With **elections** every five years, most politicians focus on policies that will have an effect within their term of office. Supply-side policies with real potential to increase prosperity may be underfunded – such as infrastructure and education and training.

● Some supply-side policies have worked better than others. Some increase inequality, creating controversy.

● The **CMA** can be very successful in promoting competition, which creates an incentive to increase efficiency and productivity and cut prices. However, competition law may not be enforced as strongly as it could be. Tackling vested interests can be difficult.

● **Working tax credits** have created an incentive to work. The policy has been very successful (see page 48). But it has allowed employers to offer very low pay. This means that it is costly for the government. Chancellor Osborne tackled the problem by raising minimum wage rates. Watch the news to see how this works out.

● **Flexible working practices** suit some but may not help those who need to work full-time.

Trade barriers

● Over time, **reducing trade barriers** has been very successful in opening up new markets for exporters and providing cheap consumer goods. But some people oppose them.

Weaknesses are easy to identify. However, many supply-side policies have been very useful already and some could be more so if governments planned for the long run.

Potential policy conflicts and trade-offs facing policy-makers when applying policies

Austerity

● From 2010-16, the government had a strong preference for austerity. The intention was to pay off the large government deficit that followed the bailing out of the banks in the financial crisis, 2008-9. The focus was on cutting government expenditure. So some expensive supply-side policies (e.g. education and R&D) were less well funded. There was a trade off between short and long term policies.

● The problem with paying off a deficit has always been that it requires higher taxes and lower government spending. These are contractionary policies – they will lead to slower growth and more unemployment, which reduces tax revenue. This makes it harder to pay off the deficit and means that the recession lasts longer. The trade-off is between recovery from the recession and paying off the debt.

● Reducing benefits may create an incentive to work but this may create poverty and social problems. There is a trade-off between the two. Social problems can be expensive in the long run.

● Flexible labour markets can allow businesses to make more people redundant.

Deregulation

● Making life easier for businesses by **deregulating** may lead to deteriorating working conditions in some companies. It might work well if all employers took CSR seriously. (There is less regulation in the UK than in most other developed countries.)

4.4.4 The impact of macroeconomic policies

The theoretical effects of macroeconomic policies have already been covered. In practice, the success of any policy depends on an accurate assessment of the state of the economy and current objectives. With that information you should be able to work out some likely consequences.

Data matters

Much also depends on whether unexpected developments occur.

● Before the EU referendum in June 2016, the MPC was considering raising interest rates. This would have been the first change since 2009, when very low interest rates became the norm because all the developed countries were going into recession.

● After the referendum, uncertainty about the future of the UK economy caused an exchange rate depreciation of around 11%. Raising the base rate was put on hold. (See pages 13-14 if you need to revise the effects of depreciation.) Two months after the referendum base rate was reduced to 0.25%.

● Because no one yet knows what UK trading relationships will look like after Brexit, prediction is difficult. In this situation we can still work out what might happen – but we have to study a range of possible scenarios.

● Other events that can change the direction of policy include new technologies (think, robots), oil price changes, political changes, unstable banking systems… and so on.

● Events in trading partners' economies may impact on any other trading partner – they are interdependent.

> **Try this**
> Practice drawing AS/AD diagrams. Start with the impact on the UK economy of the oil price fall that started in mid-2014 and continued into 2016. Then try showing the consequences of depreciation. This will require a diagram for the short run and another for the long run (i.e. after 2 years have elapsed). Again, compare notes with fellow-students. If your conclusions differ ask a teacher or any other handy economist. Good diagrams may differ but still offer useful insights.

The Brexit process (when it starts) is expected to cause slower economic growth.

The Autumn Statement 2016 – changes in macro-economic policies

● Chancellor Hammond stayed fairly close to his predecessor's policies. But he made two changes:

● The focus was still on paying off the deficit, but not quite so quickly. Instead of Mr Osborne's target of a budget surplus by 2019-20, Mr Hammond's target was for the annual deficit to be below 2% of GDP by 2020-21. This is much more realistic.

● Mr Hammond's other change was to reduce corporation tax to 17% by 2020. (Mr Osborne cut corporation tax from 28% in 2010 to 20% in 2015. This led to a loss of £8 billion in tax revenue.)

Brexit and uncertainty

● These changes reflected the impact of Brexit. Lower business taxes can create an incentive to invest. This is an expansionary policy. However it may not work. UK business profits in 2016 were the highest since 1998 and unemployment was at an all-time low.

> **Think!**
> The Brexit process (when it starts) is expected to cause slower economic growth. Initially the forecast for 2017 was for 2.2% growth. The Office of Budget Responsibility suggested a fall to 1.4%, i.e. still growing but rather more slowly.
>
> 1. How would this change affect a) investment and b) tax revenue?
> 2. Compare the forecasts above with what is actually happening.
> 3. How does the economy look now?

Notice that policy change means creating a policy package that can address a range of issues. Be prepared to examine how and why the economic situation is changing over time.

Comparing alternative approaches

● Some economic decisions are based on what we know about the way economies work. They reflect skilled understanding of economic trends. They may not be politically controversial, although some people may in fact not understand them, (especially if they have never studied a course like this one).

Political views

- Other decisions may be based on the political situation. Some conservatives favour 'small government'. This would apply to the USA from 2017 and the UK between 2010 and 2016. A key feature of this approach would be cutting both taxes and government expenditure.

- More left-leaning governments (like the Labour government, 1997-2010) will tend to spend more, on welfare, schools, care in the community and environmental issues. Taxes might rise to allow this. They might also adopt **Keynesian policies**, which are more interventionist.

Keynesians

- J.M. Keynes studied the economy of the 1930s, the time of the Great Depression. He observed that the economy could be stimulated by increasing government spending and lower taxes, borrowing to make that possible. In time, tax revenues increased so that the deficit could be paid off.

Monetarists

The conservative government of 1979-1997 began with **monetarist policies**. The idea was to use highly contractionary policies to reduce inflation. This was a success but it involved high unemployment, slow economic growth and falling incomes, over a long period. During the 90s, the economy began to grow steadily. This was the beginning of the Great Moderation, which lasted until 2007.

Monetarist and Keynesian views can be seen in the debate over austerity, which has some connections to monetarism. Those who want to delay paying off the deficit are thinking along Keynesian lines, stimulating the economy and collecting more tax revenue because unemployment will be less of a problem and recessions will be shorter.

Automatic stabilisers can work. When the economy is in recession, the government spends more on unemployment benefits and accepts lower tax revenue because incomes are depressed. This leads to a larger public deficit. When there is fast growth, tax revenue rises and with fewer people unemployed, benefits cost less. A surplus may be within reach. These trends can be observed in the phases of the economic cycle.

Identifying criteria for success and evaluating effectiveness

Success is usually taken to mean steady economic growth, low unemployment, low inflation, high investment and exports, with moderate imports, so that the trade balance is stable. Other important objectives could include high and rising productivity, technical innovation, strong competition, reducing inequality, a sustainable environment, quality education and healthcare and so on.

The priorities attached to these objectives depend heavily on political opinions. So effectiveness depends on what the expectations for each individual policy actually are. A key factor is the care with which a government constructs its policy package and the extent to which it pays attention to trade-offs.

Unintended consequences

Good government requires that political parties guard against unintended consequences and false economies. Effectiveness depends upon:

- Knowing the likely consequences of each policy and taking into account the other components of the policy package.

Example
Governments that try to increase economic growth need to be sure that they will not go so far as to stoke up inflation. Governments that want to detach themselves from trade agreements may be surprised by how much this will close off important export markets and raise import prices.

- Even if a policy has met its original objectives, it may have had negative effects on other areas of the economy.

Tax cuts may please taxpayers but if they go together with a cut in benefits, serious social problems may arise so that some neighbourhoods become less safe and children's basic needs for health care and education may be neglected. The resulting problems may be very costly in the long run.

4.5

Chapter 11
Risk and the financial sector

Terms to revise: risks and uncertainty occur in many different contexts in Themes 1 and 2 – use the index in the Year 1 revision guide. Exchange rates, (RG Theme 2, pages 92-3 and 108), the role of the banking system, (RG Theme 1, pages 32-7), inflation, (RG Theme 2, pages 99-101).

4.5.1 Risks and uncertainty

Probabilities

Risks can be quantified. This is what insurance companies do – they calculate the level of risk for the customer who wants to buy insurance. Travel insurance gets more costly as people get older because insurance companies can calculate how much more likely they are to require medical care while they are away, using past data as a guide. Businesses study risk factors when planning future developments.

Uncertainty is different – it is impossible to predict.

● There is no way for us to predict the price of oil in two years time because we do not know how many new sources of oil will be discovered, whether war in the Middle East will cut production or whether demand will fall if new vehicles turn out to be less thirsty.

● Predicting profit levels is difficult for any business. They may have a target but any change in the business environment can cause deviation from the target. Changes in government policies, changes in customer preferences, innovative technologies that a competing business may adopt, can all affect sales. Changes in input costs can affect profit too.

● Uncertainty makes it difficult for businesses and governments to plan for the future.

The impact of shocks

Shocks are unexpected events that cannot be predicted but have a significant effect on one or more economies. The reunification of Germany at the end of the Cold War involved very considerable adaptation for both East and West Germany because their standards of living were very different.

● The fall in **commodity prices** generally in 2014-15 (including oil) was a major setback for economies that depend on exporting commodities for much of their income.

● Brazil, oil exporters including Russia, and many African economies that depend on exports of minerals such as copper, were all seriously affected.

● The **financial crisis of 2007-9** had global effects because the banking system failed to function normally for many months.

● Uncertainty makes businesses very reluctant to **invest** and FDI slows. The fall in injections can be very significant.

Adjustment

● Shocks always require considerable **adjustment** for people, businesses and governments. The length of time involved varies but is almost always a matter of years. Germany adapted to the 1989 reunification slowly over many years; unemployment is still higher in the east than in the west.

> **Think!**
> How would falling export revenues affect the economies concerned?
>
> How would businesses be affected when banks stopped lending?
>
> Use AS/AD diagrams to help explain both situations.

Exchange rate risk and forward markets

Exchange rates are often volatile. They are changing all the time, every second. There are considerable risks for businesses that need to exchange currencies. But they can insure against potential losses by using **forward markets**.

> **Forward markets** make it possible to buy a certain quantity of goods or foreign currency at a price agreed today, for delivery at a specific future date. This makes it possible to insure against unexpected changes in prices or exchange rates.

- Import businesses can buy the amount of foreign currency that they need to pay for a delivery in a certain number of months. This means that the price they will have to pay is fixed; it removes all uncertainty.

- Similarly, businesses that need to buy imported commodities can buy in forward markets. The London Metal Exchange can agree to sell copper that is used in electrical products at a specific price for delivery at a certain time in the future.

Currencies and commodities

- There are forward markets for all raw or semi-processed commodities. Also, farmers can sell their crops for a fixed price now, for delivery after the harvest.

- Forward markets allow businesses to plan ahead without fear of major changes in prices or exchange rates. The period of a forward contract may be one or a few months, up to a year.

The role of insurance in business

> **Insurance** is the principle by which risks are shared between all those who wish to protect themselves from unforeseen outcomes.

Sharing risks

Individuals and businesses all face risks. We pay a premium that reflects the likelihood of the risk occurring. In return we receive compensation when the insured risk actually occurs. By sharing the risks we can prevent difficulties from creating catastrophic problems.

- Insurance companies have to have large reserves to cover the possibility of many customers requiring compensation all at once. They invest these reserves very carefully, themselves spreading the risk that some investments may not be profitable.

- They buy shares, government bonds (loans) and other financial products. They are therefore important sources of investment finance, playing a big part in the funding of both public and private sector projects.

- Businesses are able to function because they can insure against serious misfortunes that might threaten their survival (e.g. fire or theft). Insurance is a cost of production and should be reflected in the prices charged.

4.5.2 The role of the financial sector

Finance is all about providing a safe place for savings and lending to businesses, individuals and governments. Lending can be for a very specific purpose or it can be for general expenditure, e.g. governments borrowing to fund a public sector deficit, or consumers borrowing on their credit cards just to get what they want now.

Mobilising savings for lending to firms and individuals

- Saving is all about having money in the future. Savings may be kept to cover unexpected difficulties in the future or until there is enough money to pay for something specific like an exotic holiday, a housing purchase or a new container vessel.

Saving

● Savings need to be kept safe. Keeping cash 'under the mattress' is not smart. It earns no interest; it is not put to work. Businesses save retained profits to help fund future investment projects.

Financial intermediaries

● Investment banks, retail banks and building societies are all safe places to keep money. They are financial intermediaries that can invest by providing loans for business and government projects. They can spread the risks associated with investments and business activity between a large number of depositors.

● Investors pay interest rates that reflect the level of risk involved in their projects. Individuals similarly pay interest rates that reflect their personal financial history. (If they have failed to pay off debts in the past, they will pay very high interest rates or be unable to get a loan at all.)

● Banks make their money by charging higher interest rates for loans than they pay in interest to savers. The difference must cover the risk of default and their administrative costs.

Interest rates

● Interest rates for savers are typically low, (from 2009-16, miniscule). That may change.

If individuals have failed to pay off debts in the past, they will pay very high interest rates or be unable to get a loan at all.

Find out
What has happened to interest rates since 2016? How have the changes affected individuals and businesses?

Lending to business for investment in working capital

Businesses typically have to cover all kinds of costs before they can sell the product. Inputs usually have to be paid for immediately. There must be enough working capital to cover the wages and salaries that must be paid each month.

Loans and overdrafts

Companies that sell mainly to other businesses (B2B) need much more working capital than, say, retailers. Normal practice requires them to invoice when the job has been completed and many customers will pay only after 60 days have elapsed since receipt of invoices. Banks provide both loans and overdrafts. The latter usually require higher interest rates, but there will be times when they are not needed.

Lending to individuals

Individuals need to borrow for major purchases such as housing and vehicles. If their bank trusts them because they have a good credit rating, they may be allowed a loan or an overdraft just to cover current spending.

Interest rates may be quite high because they reflect the borrower's personal financial history. (If they have failed to pay off debts in the past, they will pay very high interest rates or be unable to get a loan at all.)

Facilitating the exchange of goods and services

● Markets are the medium through which goods and services are bought and sold. Banks provide payments mechanisms that are safe and reliable.

● The banks provide debit cards and sometimes credit cards.

Payment systems

- With bank transfers taking over from cheques, payment systems are becoming quicker and cheaper too. This applies to international payments as well as domestic ones.

- For most people and small businesses banking services are largely free, but the banks make money out of less commonly used services such as international payments.

- Banks are rather more efficient than they used to be; IT systems have made big changes possible.

Assessing creditor risk

In the past, individuals sometimes made loans independently, e.g. for mortgages. Without a bank or building society as an intermediary, they could get a better rate of return for themselves. However this was very risky because individuals are not usually in a position to evaluate the risks associated with individual borrowers, who may go on to default on the debt.

Credit and risk

Banks have developed considerable expertise in assessing the risk-worthiness of creditors (i.e. potential borrowers). They are helped by **credit reference agencies** (sometimes known as rating agencies, e.g. Experian). Banks and credit reference agencies typically share information all the time. They may gather information from courts and bankruptcy proceedings, hire-purchase companies and professional debt collectors. If you get into debt, they will know.

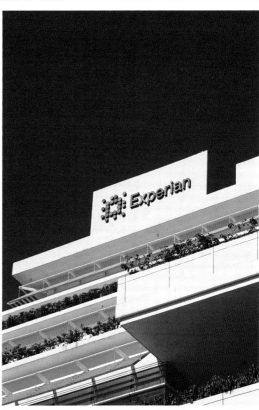

In this way, banks can assess the **probability** that a loan will not be paid back. With this information, they can accurately assess the level of **reserves** they need to allow for losses. This is an important part of their function as financial intermediaries between savers and borrowers.

Credit reference agencies such as Experian assess the risk-worthiness of potential borrowers.

This is the theory and mostly it works quite well. However for a few years before the **financial crisis**, many banks failed to notice that the rating agencies were overlooking some weaknesses in the system. They were taken in by new types of financial products that supposedly spread risks among many lenders and were therefore safe. In the event there were many more defaults than expected. For further detail go to page 109, (speculation and market bubbles).

Providing forward markets in currencies and commodities

Banks can help businesses to use forward markets and reduce risks. They arrange contracts to purchase currency or commodities in the forward market. These are known as futures. Using forward markets may be referred to as hedging.

Providing a market for equities

PLCs

Stock exchanges are the actual markets for equities (shares in a PLC). But moves to modernise the financial markets led to most stockbrokers being taken over by banks. They now act as buyers and sellers for their customers. Investment banks are very often involved in helping businesses that want to become PLCs, i.e. to be listed on the stock exchange. Banks may also offer services facilitating mergers and takeovers.

4.5.3 The role of the central bank

 WATCH OUT!

Make sure you understand the section on monetary policy, pages 92-3.

Remember that 'the Bank' means the Bank of England. No other UK bank has the capital letter.

The role of the Monetary Policy Committee in setting the official interest (base) rate

The MPC

The MPC consists of nine very expert economists who spend almost their entire time watching the data before they reach a joint conclusion, at their meeting each month. The committee includes the Governor of the Bank of England and four of its highest level officers, and four external members. Until 1997, the government of the day chose when to change the base rate. At that point there was growing evidence that monetary policy worked better if the central bank was independent of the government. This meant that politicians could not manipulate interest rates just to bolster their chances of winning an election. In 1997, right after the election of the Labour government, the Bank of England was made independent and the MPC was set up.

Transparency

● Transparency is guaranteed because the minutes of MPC meetings are always made public two weeks later.

● The 2% target rate of inflation is symmetrical. If inflation is deviating by more than 1% either way, the Governor of the Bank must write a letter of explanation to the Chancellor.

● Inflation below 1% indicates that there is a danger of deflation (average prices falling). This can be dangerous: people anticipate that prices will fall further and therefore reduce spending on both investment and consumer goods.

● This leads inevitably towards recession and can be very hard to reverse. (Japan has had this problem for many years.)

● Inflation above 2% indicates that it may be accelerating, which can harm competitiveness and destabilise the economy.

Stability

● The whole point of the MPC and the 2% target is to maintain stability in the economy. Steady, small price increases help to make the economy more flexible, creating the conditions for maintaining sustainable economic growth rates.

The implementation of monetary policy to control inflation

Inflation starts to accelerate when aggregate demand is greater than aggregate supply. There will be obvious skill shortages as businesses try to recruit more staff. If they raise wages to attract more employees, costs will increase and many will then raise prices. In any case, high AD means that firms can raise prices and still sell their products.

Raising interest rates

● Higher pay and perhaps higher profits will further increase AD, as will the fact that fewer and fewer people will be unemployed. **Contractionary policies** will be considered and for central banks, that means raising base rate. This will push up interest rates right across the economy.

● This will affect businesses by raising the cost of any investment that requires loan finance. It affects consumers who need loans for big purchases, reducing their spending power.

● People with mortgages will have to make higher monthly payments; this leaves them with less **disposable income** to spend on other things. So some businesses will experience falling demand and lower profits.

Policy packages

● Some employees will be made redundant; their spending power may be greatly reduced.

● These trends will reduce aggregate demand (AD). Existing businesses will find themselves fighting to keep their sales from falling and many will compete on price. Gradually, with a time lag of up to two years, the inflation rate will be reduced.

● In practice, monetary policy will be part of a policy package that may include **fiscal** or **supply-side measures** as well.

If AD is less than AS, these policies can be reversed. If low interest rates fail to stimulate the economy, quantitative easing could be a useful additional policy. (See pages 92-3.)

Seriously high rates of inflation occurred in the 1980s and early 90s. (See Figure 1.) Since the Bank of England became independent, the expectation has been that the MPC can head off accelerating inflation before it becomes a serious problem. That could change in response to the effects of depreciation.

Figure 1: CPI – Consumer Prices Index (% change)

Source: ONS

Cost pressures

Notice that at the beginning of 2016, inflation was near to zero. By the end of 2016, it was 1.2%. It is forecast to rise to 3.5% in 2017. Bear in mind that if oil and energy prices are changing, they too will have a significant effect on the rate of inflation.

With the effect of depreciation, the MPC is likely to have a hard time maintaining stability in the run-up to Brexit. However the OECD forecasts that UK GDP growth will slow down to 1% in 2017. Rising inflation may then be due to cost pressures rather than aggregate demand.

> ### ⚠ WATCH OUT!
>
> If the problem is cost inflation, rather than excess aggregate demand, it may be much harder to control with monetary policy. If unemployment is already quite high, higher interest rates may raise unemployment further.

> **Find out**
> Get the current data for GDP growth and inflation. Were these forecasts accurate? How does the current situation look now? Can you trace the causes of current changes?

Regulation of the banking industry: the Bank of England's Financial Policy Committee

Regulating banks

Banks have always been regulated to some degree. The reason for this is that a bank failure has very detrimental effects on the economy, so we need to be as sure as we can be that this will not happen.

> **Q What happens when a bank fails?**

The basic problem is loss of confidence. Banks work on the assumption that there will never be a situation in which all their depositors want to withdraw their money. Normally this is a reasonable assumption. It enables the banks to lend large sums to finance investment projects that will help to increase the capacity of the economy and foster economic growth.

But if the bank's accounts show that a number of borrowers have been unable to pay the interest on their loans, or to repay the loan when required, it will be obvious that the bank is making losses. Depositors will

A run on the bank

realise that the bank may be short of cash. At that point they may start to withdraw their deposits. If queues form outside the bank, all the depositors will know that they need to get their savings out fast. At that point the bank fails.

Some depositors will not get their money back. This is very detrimental indeed for the economy. Individuals and businesses that have lost money will feel cheated; more significantly, their spending power will be greatly reduced and they in turn may be unable to repay their debts. A domino effect may build up right across the economy. In 2008 the UK government bailed out RBS and Lloyds Bank to prevent them from failing.

After the financial crisis, 2008-9, it became clear that banks needed to be more tightly regulated. During the crisis many banks were bailed out by their governments. This had very serious consequences for their economies, and lead to widespread recessions.

Q How does regulation work?

Cash reserves

Banks that lose money become less able to support business lending. They must be compelled to hold larger reserves of cash so that they can withstand defaults by their borrowers. To maintain a level playing field in global banking, governments have agreed on basic rules, helped by the IMF and the Bank for International Settlements. Each individual country decides the exact level of reserves that it believes to be necessary, above the agreed minimum.

The Bank of England set up the Financial Policy Committee (FPC) in 2013. *"The Committee is charged with a primary objective of identifying, monitoring and taking action to remove or reduce systemic risks with a view to protecting and enhancing the resilience of the UK financial system. The FPC has a secondary objective to support the economic policy of the Government."* Source: Bank of England

FPC

● The FPC includes the Governor of the Bank of England, four deputy governors and five external experts. Its expertise covers both financial regulation and economic policy. Its quarterly meetings focus on the long view rather than day-to-day changes. It is concerned with **macroprudential regulation**.

● Financial stability and resilience are the primary objectives. Banking regulations must be implemented and capable of preventing significant bank failures. The FPC also aims to support government policy.

● At its meetings the FPC reviews recent changes in the UK economy. In 2016 it stressed the significance of uncertainties that affected many UK economic issues.

In 2008 the UK government bailed out RBS and Lloyds Bank to prevent them from failing.

Banker to the banks – lender of last resort

An important central bank function is to act as lender of last resort. This means:

- Providing short-terms loans to even out daily fluctuations in flows of money between banks, and

- Lending to banks that are unable to meet all customer demands to withdraw their money. This occurs when a bank is close to the point of failure.

Creating confidence

The lender of last resort function helps to create confidence in the banking system – it makes it very unlikely that depositors will lose their money. But it could not prevent the financial crisis – only stop it from getting any worse.

4.5.4 The Global Financial Crisis

The financial crisis of 2008-9 had its roots in a number of different trends that combined to make it a highly dramatic event. The years of 'the Great Moderation' had led to complacency and a sense that current developments made lending much less risky than before.

Sub-prime mortgages

- Up to 2006, many banks were making good profits from mortgage loans to people with low incomes and weak credit histories, who would be unable to make the payments if they lost their jobs. This was called the sub-prime market.

- Many banks seem to have thought that housing prices would rise indefinitely and interest rates would stay low, making it easy for sub-prime borrowers to make the payments.

- The banks devised new, profitable financial products, bundling together mortgages with a variety of risks. They sold them as securities with a triple-A credit rating (i.e. very low risk). The idea was to spread the risks on the basis that there would not be widespread defaults.

- In late 2006, many economies were growing unsustainably fast (3% in the UK). Inflation was rising, and interest rates with it. This slowed the US economy; unemployment rose and redundancies caused a fall in mortgage payments and rising defaults. Many homes were left empty and housing prices fell. This continued through 2007 in many economies.

- The banks that had bought the new financial products, thinking they were profitable, quickly got into trouble. The first in the UK was Northern Rock, which suffered a classic 'run on the bank', with long queues of depositors standing on the pavement, just as they did the last time a UK bank failed in 1866. Northern Rock looked likely to fail.

A bailout

- Northern Rock applied to the Bank of England for a loan. In 2008 it was bought by the government; it eventually became part of Virgin Money. The shareholders lost their assets but the depositors got their money back.

- Ensuring that depositors get their money back is critical because it avoids people and businesses being made bankrupt and depressing the economy further.

- The problem started in the USA but excessive lending in Europe made the situation worse.

Moral hazard (too big to fail)

The fact that banks can borrow from their central banks can encourage them to take risks and behave irresponsibly. This is **moral hazard**.

A big bank will have many depositors. Many businesses that lose their deposits will be forced to cut output and employment or close down. Individuals who lose their deposits or their jobs will have to cut back their spending. This will lead very quickly to huge income losses and the collapse of aggregate demand. The bank will be '**too big to fail**'.

Moral hazard

> **Moral hazard** occurs when a person or an organisation has no incentive to act prudently or honestly because they will not have to pay for their mistakes.
>
> '**Too big to fail**' means that the cost to the whole economy of a big bank failing is so great that the government cannot allow it to happen. The bank will have to be bailed out with huge loans.

The collapse of lending to businesses

Lehman

In September 2008 Lehman, a very big US bank, collapsed and immediately closed down. It had been heavily involved in sub-prime lending. The US regulators let it go – by this time they were worrying about moral hazard and needed to make an example somewhere. But it was a mistake, because it destabilised the whole global banking system. It destroyed banks' trust so that they did not dare to lend to each other.

Normally banks lend to each other all the time, often to cover short term transactions that vary from day to day. But after the Lehman collapse, there was panic in the money markets. For several weeks most banks lent nothing at all to anyone. The fragility of the system meant that any lending was risky. The banks did not have enough reserves of cash to absorb any more losses.

Insufficient reserves

In the UK, RBS and Lloyds Bank had to be bailed out, precisely because they were too big to fail. Lehman had been an important lender for RBS. Businesses that needed to borrow to pay wages or other costs could not, and the damage was serious. You have seen what happened in the GDP data.

Speculation and market bubbles

Speculation means buying or selling something in the expectation of a price change that generates profit. Banks that bought financial products just to make a profit on selling them were in trouble if the price actually fell.

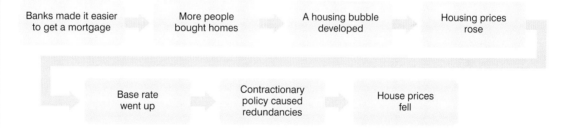

Speculation can cause market bubbles or make them worse. Speculators can buy houses and push up the price; the bubble bursts when some of them sell to get the profit. The same can happen with shares or commodities.

The role of organisational culture

Bonuses

Banking cultures were all about making a profit. Bankers received bonuses in proportion to the profits they made on their deals, giving them a big incentive to press forward with more and more risky transactions. The focus was on short term profit rather than long term prudence.

● Historically banks had been seen as prioritising safety and avoiding risks. In the 1980s and 90s, very gradually, this changed.

Speculators can buy houses and push up the price; the bubble bursts when some of them sell to get the profit.

Incentives

● Bankers developed complex models that devised new ways of spreading risks. For a while, this worked. But when economic growth turned down, the risks reappeared.

● Some people had been doubtful about these new strategies but the incentive to maximise bonuses meant that the other bankers did not want to know about the risks.

The role of banking regulation

Light touch regulation

In the past, banking regulation was strict. But there was little competition between banks. It was thought that lighter regulation would encourage innovation and competition, reduce bank charges and make the financial system more efficient. From 1987 onwards regulations were made to work more flexibly. The financial crisis changed all this.

● The key to safe banking is to have adequate reserves to deal with losses when they happen.

● The financial crisis revealed that banks were allowed to operate with levels of reserves that were insufficient to keep them safe.

● After 2009 there were long debates on the reform of banking regulation, both nationally and internationally. Within the EU basic rules were agreed and some governments went further to give added protection. The IMF was influential in the debates. Reserve requirements are now higher and discussions are continuing.

Reserves must be higher

● The bankers have tried to water down the proposed changes but the new regulations are still considerably stronger than before. The risks have been reduced. The IMF and central banks periodically require stress tests to ensure that each bank is capable of surviving future difficulties. This identifies the banks that need to take action.

The **Financial Conduct Authority** (**FCA**) covers the entire financial sector, not just the banks. It reports to the government and Parliament. Its main purpose is to ensure that financial institutions' customers are not misled. There have been times when a whole range of financial service providers mis-sold their products, as was the case with PPI, Payment Protection Insurance, which was sold to some people for whom it was inappropriate. There was asymmetric information at work – sellers knew more about the product than buyers.

The **Prudential Regulation Authority** is an arm of the Bank of England, charged with supervision of banks, building societies, credit unions, insurers and major investment firms. Its main objective is to ensure that no financial institution engages in reckless activity that will affect customers and threaten the stability of the financial system. It also monitors the insurance companies to ensure that policy-holders are adequately protected, and aims to promote competition.

The impact of the financial sector on economic agents and governments

Financial services are immensely important for individuals, businesses and governments. First, banks and other financial intermediaries create a safe place for savings that may be needed in the future. Second, investment is the lifeblood of the economy and lending makes it possible for businesses to thrive and for individuals to buy homes. The banking system also funds governments' short-term requirements and some long-term loans for major projects.

Confidence and trust

● However, the whole system is based on confidence and trust. If the economy is in an unstable state, confidence may evaporate and then loans become very hard to get.

Investment is the lifeblood of the economy.

● During the financial crisis, trust in the banks was very low, but equally, the banks became very wary about lending. Many businesses closed and there were widespread redundancies. Incomes fell and economic growth went into reverse.

Asymmetric information

● Many financial bodies tried to sell profitable products without fully explaining the way they would work to their customers. They have deliberately taken advantage of their asymmetric information. This was not regulated at the time; once it came to light it was stopped and the banks paid big fines.

● Even though customers have often been compensated, banking cultures continue to encourage the creation of very complex products with small print that is hard for customers to take in, further damaging trust in the financial system

● The UK still has very low levels of investment because of uncertainty. Confidence in the future is weak.

● Shadow banking refers to organisations (often called hedge funds) that lend finance for investment, but are much more lightly regulated than the banks. This is because they are set up by small groups of very wealthy people and financial businesses that typically deal in financial assets which they buy and sell anytime they can see a possible profit to be made from current asset price changes.

● Because of this light regulation, shadow banks could destabilise the financial system in the future.

Theme 4 – Glossary

Absolute poverty means not having enough income to provide basic necessities and survive.

Allocation of resources – how factors of production are used to create goods and services.

Allocative efficiency is achieved when resources are used to yield the maximum benefit to everyone. It is impossible to redistribute them without making someone worse off.

Anti-competitive practices aim to reduce competition; they include price fixing and collusion.

Asymmetric information occurs when one party knows more about the product than the other.

Austerity refers to cuts in public expenditure and tax increases that reduce public borrowing.

Balance of payments: the set of accounts that show export revenue and import costs, capital movements and any other international transactions.

Bank of England is the UK's central bank; it controls monetary policy.

Barriers to entry occur when start-up costs make it difficult for new businesses to enter the industry.

A **cartel** is any agreement between businesses to reduce competition or not to compete with each other. The agreement is usually secret and may be implemented in various ways.

The **Competition and Markets Authority (CMA)** investigates UK market behaviour to ensure that all businesses are acting in line with competition policy requirements.

Consumer protection refers to regulations that protect consumers from unsafe or fraudulent purchases.

Contestable markets are characterised by easy entry, i.e. new firms can set up in business easily.

The **current account** is the part of the balance of payments that covers imports and exports.

Demand-side policies affect the economy by increasing or reducing aggregate demand.

De-merit goods are over-produced by the free market, in quantities that are greater than the optimal level for society. They are generally thought to be bad for society as a whole.

De-regulation means reducing the number of regulations that affect businesses.

A **direct tax** is taken at source and goes directly to the government, e.g. Income Tax and National Insurance Contributions.

Entry and exit refer to new businesses entering a particular market and existing businesses leaving.

EU competition policy keeps markets competitive wherever there is trade between EU member countries.

Explicit collusion occurs when there is a meeting or actual agreement between businesses to avoid competing vigorously and follow a joint strategy.

External benefits are benefits or positive side-effects imposed on a third party who is neither the producer nor the consumer.

External costs are costs or negative side-effects imposed on a third party who is neither the producer nor the consumer of the product.

Financial crisis – the period in 2007-9 when banks were endangered by excessive lending.

Fiscal policy involves changes in the levels of taxation and/or government expenditure in order to affect the level of output.

Free market policies avoid government intervention, functioning on the basis of supply and demand.

Free rider problem occurs when public goods are under-provided or not provided at all because individuals are able to consume the good by paying little or nothing towards the cost.

Full capacity output is the most that the economy can produce without an increase in the factors of production.

Geographic immobility occurs when unemployed people cannot move to places where there are job vacancies.

The **Gini coefficient** measures income inequality. A coefficient of 0 would mean income is shared equally between all individuals, whilst a coefficient of 1 would mean one person within the population has all the income and everyone else none. The higher the Gini coefficient, the higher the level of inequality.

Government failure occurs when government intervention makes the situation worse rather than better. In solving one problem another is created.

Imperfect markets are distorted in ways that reduce competition. They include oligopoly and imperfect competition.

Incentives – (in economics) are payments or rewards that enable or motivate a particular course of action, or count as a reason for preferring one choice to the alternatives.

Indirect taxes are added onto prices and go indirectly to the government from the seller. Examples include VAT and Excise duty.

Inequality occurs where there are large differences in incomes and wealth within the society.

Innovation refers to the development of new ideas or techniques.

Intellectual property rights are ideas or inventions that are protected by patents or copyright.

Interventionist policies are designed to control market forces, usually for political reasons.

Marginal cost (**MC**) is the cost for producing one more unit of output.

Marginal revenue (**MR**) is the extra revenue that comes from selling one more unit of output.

Market – any medium in which buyers and sellers interact and agree to trade at a price.

Market failure happens when a market does not efficiently allocate resources to achieve the greatest possible consumer satisfaction. The allocation of resources is such that a reallocation would make some people better off. (Allocative efficiency has not been reached.)

Merit goods can be provided by the private sector and often are, but the quantity that the free market provides is lower than the optimum level for society. They are under-provided by the market mechanism. Public sector activity can create an optimum level of output.

Monetary policy uses interest rates to vary the costs of borrowing and influence the level of aggregate demand.

The **Monetary Policy Committee** (**MPC**) sets interest rates and seeks to prevent inflation from changing significantly.

Moral hazard means that people take bigger risks when they know they will not personally have to cover the cost of a mistake.

A **natural monopoly** occurs when the most efficient scale of production is a monopoly. More than one producer or supplier would involve wasteful duplication of resources.

Non excludable means that it is impossible to prevent people who have not paid for a good from consuming it.

Non rivalrous means that if one person consumes a good it does not affect or reduce the amount left for someone else to consume.

Normal profit means just enough profit to enable a business to keep going.

Occupational immobility occurs when unemployed people lack the skills needed to do the jobs that are available.

Overheating occurs when aggregate demand exceeds aggregate supply and inflation is accelerating due to shortages.

Perfect competition is a model that describes markets where all products are identical (i.e. homogeneous) with no differentiation and there are many competing businesses. Only normal profit can be obtained and everyone will have perfect knowledge of the market.

The **poverty trap** is a situation in which an unemployed person would be even poorer or not much richer in work because they would no longer receive unemployment benefit.

Price discrimination means charging a higher price to people whose price elasticity of demand is low. The seller must be able to identify the groups of people who are more sensitive to prices.

Privatisation means transferring production out of the public sector and into the private sector.

Productive (or technical) efficiency maximises the effective use of resources. (See also productivity).

Profit signalling mechanism – the means by which resources are allocated. The presence of profit in a market attracts more resources and creates more output. Losses drive resources away.

A **progressive tax** is one that takes a greater percentage of income from richer people than poorer people.

The **Prudential Regulation Authority** (**PRA**) is part of the Bank of England and supervises banks, building societies and insurance companies.

A **public sector deficit** occurs when public expenditure is greater than tax revenue; the deficit is covered by borrowing.

A **public good** is one that the free market will not provide at all. There is no incentive for a producer to supply it, it is impossible to charge for it and make a profit and it is impossible to prevent anyone else from consuming it for free.

The **public interest** is a loose term but means the welfare or wellbeing of the public in general, as opposed to the selfish interests of individuals, groups and businesses. In the context of this course it means the interests of consumers in general rather than businesses.

Redistribution refers to the use of tax revenue to raise the standard of living of poorer people.

Regulations are legal and other rules that apply to businesses. They may come from governments, the EU or trade associations.

A **regulatory body** is a public authority or government agency responsible for enforcing government regulations.

Regulatory capture happens when the regulator is more influenced by the industry's point of view than the consumer's.

Relative poverty exists when someone does not have enough income to participate fully in the society in which they live.

Research and development (**R&D**) helps to develop products or processes that are new, better or cheaper.

Restrictive practices include any action that a business uses to limit competition.

Shocks are unexpected events that affect the economy and often come from outside it. They are not predictable.

Social benefits are the total benefits of producing goods and services and are calculated by adding together the private and external benefits.

Social costs are the total costs of producing goods and services and are calculated by adding together the private and external costs.

Supply-side policies include all measures designed to increase the productive capacity of the economy. They influence aggregate supply rather than aggregate demand.

Tacit collusion (or tacit agreement) occurs when competing firms appear to follow a similar strategy to reach the same aim, such as avoiding price cutting, but without meeting or having any kind of agreement.

Trade (X-M) is the difference between exports, which are part of the overall demand for UK produced products, and imports which are not produced in the UK.

Tradable pollution permits allow some businesses to pollute the atmosphere up to a certain level but no more. The total allowed can be reduced over time, allowing businesses to reduce their polluting processes gradually. If the business cuts pollution faster than it needs to, it can sell its unused permits to another business. This creates an incentive to reduce pollution.

Trade-offs occur when two objectives cannot both be achieved. The more you have of one variable the less you have of the other.

Vacancies are unfilled jobs; when they increase it is likely that there are skill shortages.

Index